Workkeys Test (NCRC) Applied Math Practice Test Book Study Guide for Preparation for the Workkeys Exam

The Workkeys examination is a trademark of ACT Inc, which is not affiliated with nor endorses this publication.

Workkeys Test (NCRC) Applied Math Practice Test Book: Study Guide for Preparation for the Workkeys Exam

© COPYRIGHT 2018

Exam SAM Study Aids & Media dba www.examsam.com

All rights reserved. No part of this publication may be reproduced, stored in a retrieval system, or transmitted, in any form or by any means, electronic, mechanical, photocopying, recording, or otherwise, without the prior written permission of the copyright owner.

ISBN-13: 978-0-9998087-6-4

ISBN-10: 0-9998087-6-1

The Workkeys examination is a trademark of ACT Inc, which is not affiliated with nor endorses this publication.

How to Use This Publication

You should work through the concepts and practice questions for levels 3 to 7 in sections 1 to 5 of the study guide first. Pay special attention to the tips and hints after each question in sections 1 to 5. They tell you how to solve each type of question that you will see on the real test and give you strategies for the day of your exam. Then attempt each of the other practice tests for levels 3 to 7.

The mixed-level practice tests simulate the actual exam experience, so attempt the mixed-level practice tests after you have studied all of the other material in the book. To simulate the real exam, you should allow 55 minutes to take each of the mixed-level practice tests.

On the real exam, you will be allowed to use a calculator and scratch paper to solve the problems. On the real test, you will not be penalized for guessing, so you should try to answer every question.

The answers and solutions for all of the practice tests are provided at the end of the last practice exam.

This study guide assumes some knowledge of basic math skills, such as addition, subtraction, multiplication, division, percentages, and decimals.

If you have difficulties with basic math problems or if you have been out of school for a while, you may wish to review our free basic math problems before taking the practice tests in this book.

The free review problems can be found at: www.examsam.com/math/numerical-skills/

TABLE OF CONTENTS

How to Use This Publication i

Workkeys Practice Test 1 – Level 3

Adding Whole Numbers 1

Subtracting Whole Numbers 1

Multiplying Whole Numbers 1

Dividing Whole Numbers 1

Adding Negative Numbers 2

Subtracting Negative Numbers 2

Changing Fractions to Decimals 2

Changing Decimals to Percentages 3

Changing Fractions to Percentages 3

Changing Decimals to Fractions 3

Changing Percentages to Fractions 3

Changing Percentages to Decimals 4

Units of Money 4

Units of Time 4

Workkeys Practice Test 2 – Level 4

Problems with Two or More Operations 5

Negative Numbers – Multiplication 6

Averages 6

Simple Ratios 6

Simple Proportions 7

Simple Rates 7

Adding Fractions with a Common Denominator 8

Subtracting Fractions with a Common Denominator 8

Adding Commonly-Known Decimals 9

Adding Commonly-Known Percentages 9

Multiplying Mixed Numbers by Whole Numbers	9
Multiplying Mixed Numbers by Decimals	10
Putting Information in Order before Solving	10

Workkeys Practice Test 3 – Level 5

Fractions with Unlike Denominators	11
Identifying Errors in Calculations	11
Formulas with Conversions	11
Formulas with Measurements	12
Mixed Unit Calculations	12
Finding the Best Deal – One-Step Calculations	12
Finding the Best Deal – Two-Step Calculations	13
Circles – Area	13
Circles – Circumference	13
Rectangles – Area	13
Rectangles – Perimeter	14
Calculating Discounts	14
Calculating Markups	14

Workkeys Practice Test 4 – Level 6

Calculating Reverse Percentages	15
Converting Quantity within Systems of Measurement	15
Converting Time within Systems of Measurement	15
Identifying Why a Mistake Occurred in a Solution	16
Finding the Best Deal and Using It for Further Calculations	16
Rearranging Formula for the Area of a Circle	16
Rearranging Formula for the Area of a Rectangle	16
Converting Units of Measurement for the Area of a Circle	17
Converting Units of Measurement for the Area of a Rectangle	17
Volume of Rectangular Shape	17

Volume of a Cube 17

Calculating Production Rates by Unit 18

Calculating Production Rates by Time 18

Identifying Correct Equations to Solve Problems 18

Workkeys Practice Test 5 – Level 7

Fractions as Quantities 20

Fractions as Units 20

Decimals as Units 20

Identifying the Reason for a Mistake 21

Converting Units of Measurement – Advanced Problems 21

Determining the Best Deal – Advanced Problems 22

Volume of Spheres 22

Volume of Cylinders 22

Volume of Cones 23

Rearranging Formulas to Calculate Measurements 23

Converting Between Units of Measurement – Advanced Problems 23

Mean 24

Mode 24

Median 25

Range 25

Calculating Mean with a Missing Value 25

Mean and Median – Advanced Questions 26

Workkeys Practice Tests 6 to 15

Workkeys Practice Test 6 – Level 3 27

Workkeys Practice Test 7 – Level 4 30

Workkeys Practice Test 8 – Level 5 34

Workkeys Practice Test 9 – Level 6 37

Workkeys Practice Test 10 – Level 7 40

Workkeys Practice Test 11 – Mixed-Level	43
Workkeys Practice Test 12 – Mixed-Level	50
Workkeys Practice Test 13 – Mixed-Level	57
Workkeys Practice Test 14 – Mixed-Level	64
Workkeys Practice Test 15 – Mixed-Level	71
Answers, Solutions, and Explanations Tests 1 to 15	
Test 1 Solutions and Explanations – Level 3	77
Test 2 Solutions and Explanations – Level 4	79
Test 3 Solutions and Explanations – Level 5	81
Test 4 Solutions and Explanations – Level 6	82
Test 5 Solutions and Explanations – Level 7	84
Test 6 Solutions and Explanations – Level 3	87
Test 7 Solutions and Explanations – Level 4	88
Test 8 Solutions and Explanations – Level 5	90
Test 9 Solutions and Explanations – Level 6	91
Test 10 Solutions and Explanations – Level 7	93
Test 11 Solutions and Explanations – Mixed-Level	95
Test 12 Solutions and Explanations – Mixed-Level	99
Test 13 Solutions and Explanations – Mixed-Level	103
Test 14 Solutions and Explanations – Mixed-Level	106
Test 15 Solutions and Explanations – Mixed-Level	110
Answer Key – All Questions	114
Appendix – Applied Mathematics Formula Sheet	126

Workkeys Practice Test 1 – Level 3

Adding Whole Numbers

1) Your company sells electronics online. The annual sales for the first three years of business are: $25,135, $32,787, and $47,004. What was the total sales for the past three years?
   A) $101,326
   B) $104,916
   C) $104,926
   D) $104,944
   E) $109,426

This is a question on adding whole numbers. The problem is asking for the total for all three years, so add the three figures together.

Subtracting Whole Numbers

2) You are the cashier in a pet food store. A customer gives you $50 to pay for the items he purchased, which total $41.28. How much change should you give the customer?
   A) $7.82
   B) $8.18
   C) $8.27
   D) $8.72
   E) $9.72

This is a question on subtracting whole numbers. For questions like this that ask you to calculate the change given to a customer, you need to take the amount of money the customer gives you and subtract the amount of the purchase.

Multiplying Whole Numbers

3) As a car salesperson, you earn a $175 referral fee on every customer who accepts a customer service upgrade. You referred 8 customers for the service upgrade this month. How much did you earn in referral fees for the month?
   A) $1050
   B) $1200
   C) $1225
   D) $1256
   E) $1400

This is a question on multiplying whole numbers. Multiplication problems will often include the words 'each' or 'every.' Multiply the amount of the referral fee by the number of customers to solve.

Dividing Whole Numbers

4) Your weekly pay is $535.50 and you work 30 hours per week. How much are you paid per hour?
   A) $17.83
   B) $17.84
   C) $17.85
   D) $18.34
   E) $18.45

This is a question on dividing whole numbers. Division problems will often include the word 'per.' Divide the total weekly amount by the number of hours to solve.

Adding Negative Numbers

5) Business losses are represented as negative numbers, while business profits are represented as positive numbers. A business makes the following profits and losses during a four week period: –$286, $953, $1502, and –$107. What was the total business profit or loss during these four weeks?
A) $2,026
B) $2,062
C) $2,080
D) –$2,026
E) –$2,062

This is a question on adding negative numbers. When you have to add a negative number to a positive number, you are really subtracting. So, add the business profits and subtract the business losses to solve.

Subtracting Negative Numbers

6) Location below sea level is represented as a negative number. The location below sea level of Lake Alto is –35 meters. The location below sea level of Lake Bajo is 62 meters deeper than Lake Alto. What figure represents the location below sea level for Lake Bajo?
A) –97
B) 97
C) –62
D) –27
E) 27

This is a question on subtracting negative numbers. The facts state that the location below sea level of Lake Bajo is 62 meters deeper than Lake Alto, so we need to subtract this figure from the location below sea level of Lake Alto. The location below sea level of Lake Alto is a negative number, so you are subtracting a negative from a negative.

Changing Fractions to Decimals

7) You are working on a project and have completed 3/5 of it. What figure below expresses the project completion amount as a decimal number?
A) 0.06
B) 0.60
C) 1.67
D) 3.00
E) 6.00

This is a question on changing fractions to decimals. To express a fraction as a decimal, treat the line in the fraction as the division symbol and divide accordingly. Remember to be careful with the decimal placement in your final answer.

Changing Decimals to Percentages

8) A teacher reports attendance as a decimal figure, calculated as the number of students attending divided into the total number of students in the class. This week, the attendance was 0.55. What percentage best represents the attendance for this week?
   A) 0.55%
   B) 5.50%
   C) 55.0%
   D) 55.5%
   E) 550%

This is a question on changing decimals to percentages. To express a decimal number as a percentage, move the decimal point two places to the right. Then add the percent sign.

Changing Fractions to Percentages

9) You have used up 5/14 of your vacation days. Approximately what percentage of your vacation days have you already used?
   A) 0.357%
   B) 2.800%
   C) 3.571%
   D) 35.71%
   E) 37.51%

This is a question on changing fractions to decimals. Treat the line in the fraction as the division symbol and divide. Then move the decimal point two places to the right, and add the percent sign.

Changing Decimals to Fractions

10) You have used 0.75 of the gas you last put in your car. What fraction best represents the amount of gas you have used?
    A) 1/4
    B) 2/5
    C) 2/3
    D) 3/5
    E) 3/4

This is a question on changing a decimal number to a fraction. You should be able to recognize the equivalent decimal numbers for commonly-used fractions such as ½ or ¾ for your exam. If you are unsure, perform division on the answer choices to solve.

Changing Percentages to Fractions

11) It is reported that 33% of all new stores close within five years of opening. What fraction best represents this percentage?
    A) 1/3
    B) 1/4
    C) 1/5
    D) 2/3
    E) 2/5

This is a question on changing a percentage to a fraction. You should also be able to recognize the equivalent fractions for commonly-used percentages for the test. If you are unsure of the answer, perform division on the answer choices to solve.

Changing Percentages to Decimals

12) A carpet store is offering 45% off in a sale this month. What decimal number below best represents the percentage off?
    A) 0.0045
    B) 0.0450
    C) 0.4500
    D) 4.5000
    E) 45.000

This is a question on changing percentages to decimals. Any given percentage is out of 100%, so we divide by 100 to express a percentage as a decimal. So, move the decimal point two places to the left and remove the percent sign.

Units of Money

13) You work at a bakery and have to pay 36 cents for each pound of flour you buy. You decide to buy 14¼ pounds of flour today. How much will you have to pay?
    A) $3.60
    B) $5.13
    C) $5.31
    D) $142.50
    E) $513.00

This is a question on calculations involving units of money. Express both amounts as decimal numbers and multiply to solve.

Units of Time

14) You are a bookkeeper, and you have just been with a client for 0.35 hours. Approximately how many minutes did you spend with this client?
    A) 3.5 minutes
    B) 5.8 minutes
    C) 21 minutes
    D) 35 minutes
    E) 42 minutes

This is a question on calculations involving units of time. There are 60 minutes in an hour, so multiply the minutes in the hour by the decimal number given in the problem to solve.

Workkeys Practice Test 2 – Level 4

Problems with Two or More Operations

15) A flower store charges $24 for a small arrangement of flowers. A customer will get a $5 discount if he or she provides his or her own vase for the small arrangement. This month, there were 12 customers who ordered small arrangements and provided their own vases. How much money in total did the flower store make on arrangements sold to these 12 customers?
    A) $228
    B) $282
    C) $288
    D) $348
    E) $384

This is a question with two operations. Subtract the discount from the original price. Then multiply this figure by the number of units sold.

16) You are a bricklayer working for a construction company. You laid bricks for 7 hours per day for 4 days on one job. The customer was billed $45 per hour for your work, and you were paid $25 per hour. After your wages have been paid, how much money did the company make for your work on this job?
    A) $175
    B) $180
    C) $315
    D) $560
    E) $700

This question has three operations. First, you need to determine the total number of hours worked for the 4 days. Then calculate the profit your company makes per hour. Finally, multiply the total number of hours by the profit per hour to solve.

17) You are a pharmacist and own a local drug store. Last week, you filled 250 prescriptions in 40 hours. Assuming that each prescription takes the same amount of time, how many minutes should it take you to fill a single prescription?
    A) 0.16 minutes
    B) 1.6 minutes
    C) 3.75 minutes
    D) 6.25 minutes
    E) 9.6 minutes

This is a question with two operations. Since there are 60 minutes in an hour, we multiply by 60 to get the number of minutes. Then divide by the number of prescriptions to get the rate.

18) A truck driver delivered 120 orders this week. She delivered 105 of the orders on time. What percentage of the driver's orders was delivered on time?
    A) 0.875%
    B) 8.75%
    C) 87.5%
    D) 0.125%
    E) 12.50%

> This is a question with two operations. Take the amount of orders that were delivered on time and divide by the amount of total orders. Then convert to a percentage.

Negative Numbers – Multiplication

19) You are a scientist measuring cell growth or attrition. Each day a measurement is taken. Cell growth is represented as a positive figure, while cell attrition is represented as a negative figure. On Monday cell growth was 27, and for all days Tuesday through Friday, cell attrition was 13 per day. What number represents total cell growth or attrition for these five days?
A) 25
B) −25
C) 40
D) −40
E) 79

> This is a question on multiplying negative numbers. Cell attrition is a negative number, so perform multiplication to get the total for Tuesday through Friday. Then add the cell growth for Monday to solve.

Averages

20) A vegetable farmer works until noon each day. The chart below shows the amounts of cucumbers per hour that she picked one morning:
7:00 to 8:00   23 cucumbers
8:00 to 9:00   25 cucumbers
9:00 to 10:00   26 cucumbers
10:00 to 11:00 24 cucumbers
11:00 to 12:00 22 cucumbers

On average, how many cucumbers did the farmer pick per hour?
A) 23
B) 24
C) 25
D) 26
E) 26.5

> This is a question on calculating averages. The average is sometimes called the arithmetic mean, so you may see both terms on the test. To find the average, you need to add all of the amounts to get the total, and then divide the total by the number of hours.

Simple Ratios

21) You run a local company that makes concrete. When making one particular kind of concrete, you have to add 2 units of sand for every 3 units of cement powder. You are currently making a batch of this concrete that has 66 units of cement powder. How many units of sand should you add to this batch?
A) 2
B) 3
C) 22
D) 44
E) 66

This is a question on a simple ratio. Take the 66 units of cement powder for the current batch and divide by the 3 units stated in the original ratio. Then multiply this result by the 2 units of sand stated in the original ratio to solve.

22) It is company policy that the ratio of employees to supervisors should be 50:1. So, for every 50 employees in a company, there should be 1 supervisor. If there are 255 employees in total, how many supervisors are there?
   A) 1
   B) 2
   C) 3
   D) 5
   E) 250

This is another question on a simple ratio. The problem states that we are working with a ratio, so the employees and the supervisors form separate groups. First, add the two groups together. Then take the total amount of employees stated in the problem and divide this by the figure you have just calculated to get the amount of supervisors.

Simple Proportions

23) A report shows that 2 out of every 20 employees of a particular company are interested in applying for a promotion. If the company has 480 employees in total, how many employees are interested in applying for a promotion?
   A) 20
   B) 24
   C) 42
   D) 48
   E) 84

This is a question on a simple proportion. Problems on proportions often use the phrase 'out of.' The problem uses the phrase '2 *out of* every 20 employees' so we know that there are 2 employees who form a subset within each group of 20. So, take the total number of employees and divide this by 20. Then multiply this result by the amount in the subset to solve.

Simple Rates

24) In your job as a mechanic, you spent from 8:10 to 8:22 changing three wheel covers on a car. At this rate, how many wheel covers could you change per hour?
   A) 3
   B) 5
   C) 10
   D) 12
   E) 15

This is a question on calculating a simple rate. Calculate the amount of time in minutes that was spent on the three wheel covers. Then calculate the time in minutes needed to change 1 wheel cover. Then divide this amount into 60 minutes to solve.

Adding Fractions with a Common Denominator

25) A fencing company put up $15^2/_8$ yards of fence for one customer and $13^5/_8$ yards of fence for another customer. How many yards of fence did the company put up for both customers in total?
   A) $28^3/_8$
   B) $28^5/_8$
   C) $28^7/_8$
   D) $28^7/_{16}$
   E) $28^{10}/_{64}$

This is a question on adding fractions that have a common denominator. First, add the whole numbers that are in front of each fraction. Then add the fractions. If you have two fractions that have the same denominator, which is the number on the bottom of the fraction, you add the numerators and keep the common denominator. Then combine the new whole number and the new fraction to solve.

---

26) It is your job to fill gourmet food boxes with various products. So far today, you have filled $2^3/_8$ boxes for one order and $4^1/_8$ boxes for another order. How many total boxes have you filled so far today?
   A) $6^1/_2$
   B) $6^1/_4$
   C) $6^3/_4$
   D) $6^3/_{16}$
   E) $6^3/_{64}$

This is another question on adding fractions that have a common denominator. Follow the same steps as for the previous question, but also simplify the fraction to solve. This means that you have to reduce the numerator and denominator by dividing them by the same number, which is known as a common factor.

Subtracting Fractions with a Common Denominator

27) A customer has just placed an order to have an awning made for his front window. According to the measurements, you will need $5^3/_{16}$ yards of canvas to make the awning. However, the customer calls later to say that his initial measurement was incorrect, and you now need only $4^1/_{16}$ yards of canvas to make the awning. Which fraction below represents the amount by which the amount of canvas has been reduced?
   A) $1^1/_8$
   B) $1^1/_{16}$
   C) $1^1/_{32}$
   D) $1^3/_{16}$
   E) $1^3/_{32}$

This is a question on subtracting fractions with a common denominator. First, subtract the whole numbers, and then subtract the fractions. If you have two fractions that have the same denominator, you subtract the numerators and keep the common denominator. Then simplify the fraction. Finally, combine the whole number and the simplified fraction to solve.

Adding Commonly-Known Decimals

28) You need to place certain additives in a bottle to make your product. Your company measures each additive in decimal units, with 1 unit representing the filled bottle. The bottle contains 0.25 units of additive A, 0.50 units of additive B, and 0.10 units of additive C. Which of the following represents, in terms of units, how full the bottle currently is?
   A) 08.5
   B) 0.85
   C) 0.90
   D) 0.95
   E) 8.50

This is a question on adding commonly-known decimals. Add the three figures together to solve. Remember to be sure to put the decimal point in the correct place when you work out the solution.

Adding Commonly-Known Percentages

29) A recent survey shows that 50% of your customers rated your service as excellent and 25% rated your service as very good. What percentage below represents the total amount of customers who rated your service either excellent or very good?
   A) 25%
   B) 50%
   C) 75%
   D) 85%
   E) 95%

This is a question on adding commonly-known percentages. Simply add the percentages together to solve.

Multiplying Mixed Numbers by Whole Numbers

30) A customer has just ordered 5 units of your product. Each unit of the product takes 1¼ hours to make. How much time is needed to make this order?
   A) 5 hours and 25 minutes
   B) 5 hours and 55 minutes
   C) 6 hours and 4 minutes
   D) 6 hours and 15 minutes
   E) 6 hours and 25 minutes

This is a question on multiplying a mixed number by a whole number of units. First, multiply the whole numbers. Then multiply the whole number of units by the fraction. Then convert this improper fraction to a mixed number. Add the whole number and the mixed number, and convert to hours and minutes to solve.

Multiplying Mixed Numbers by Decimals

31) The distance to travel to your client's premises is 100.75 miles there and 100.75 miles back. You have completed this round-trip two times already this month, and you are 1/2 of the way there on another trip when you stop at a gas station. Approximately how many miles have you traveled to this client's premises for the month in total when you stop at the gas station?
A) 202
B) 251
C) 403
D) 453
E) 504

This is a question on multiplying a mixed number by a decimal number. Take the amount of miles for a single trip and express as a decimal number. Then calculate the number of one-way trips that have already been completed or are in progress, and express this as a mixed number. Then multiply the decimal number by the mixed number to solve.

Putting Information in Order before Solving

32) You own a shoe store and have just realized that 50 pairs of shoes have been sold this month. You always like to have 75 pairs of shoes available in stock. You started the month with 95 pairs of shoes in stock. Now you need to replenish your stock. Which item below best represents the starting point for solving this problem?
A) number of shoes sold
B) desired amount of stock
C) number of shoes at the beginning of the month
D) number of units needed to replenish stock
E) the cost of the shoes from the supplier

This is a question on how to put information in the correct logical order. Remember that for questions on inventory, it is usually best to start with the beginning balance for the time period in the question.

Workkeys Practice Test 3 – Level 5

Fractions with Unlike Denominators

33) You work as a dressmaker in a tailoring shop and are trying to decide what setting to use on the sewing machine. You have tried the 1/8 inch stitch but have realized that it is too small. The stitches on the machine are sized in 1/32 increments. What size stitch should you try next?
A) 3/16
B) 5/32
C) 6/16
D) 6/32
E) 8/32

This is a question on performing calculations on fractions with different denominators. Convert 1/8 to the following equivalent fraction: 1/8 = ?/32

Identifying Errors in Calculations

34) You are a manager in a customer service telephone center. All customers must take a survey when they finish each call and state whether they were satisfied or dissatisfied with the service they received. You are reviewing the data below from the call shift that has just finished. If there is a mistake in the calculations, which row is it in?

Row	Hour	Total Customers	Satisfied Customers	Dissatisfied Customers
1	8:00 to 9:00	279	274	5
2	9:00 to 10:00	211	205	6
3	10:00 to 11:00	214	198	15
4	11:00 to 12:00	252	248	4

A) Row 1
B) Row 2
C) Row 3
D) Row 4
E) There is no mistake.

This is a question on identifying errors in a report or other calculation. Add the amounts in the last two columns for each of the rows to check the total amounts.

Formulas with Conversions

35) In your job as a lab assistant, you must fill a tank with a chemical. The volume of the tank is 60 cubic yards. Reports on the chemical are completed in cubic feet. How many cubic feet of chemical will you need in order to fill the tank?
A) 180
B) 360
C) 540
D) 1080
E) 1620

For questions on converting formulas, be sure to check the formula sheet first of all. A formula sheet like the one you will receive for the exam in provided in the appendix at the end of this book. From the formula sheet, we can see that 1 cubic yard = 27 cubic feet. To solve, multiply the amount of cubic yards by 27.

Formulas with Measurements

36) As a land surveyor, you must measure the distance between landmarks. You have measured a distance between two landmarks and discovered that it is 538 feet. What is the approximate distance between the landmarks in terms of meters?
   A) 45
   B) 164
   C) 1367
   D) 1765
   E) 6456

This is a question on using a formula with a measurement. From the formula sheet, we can see that 1 foot = 0.3048 meters. Multiply to solve.

Mixed Unit Calculations

37) In your work as a physical therapist, you measure how far your clients are able to walk during each session. One client walked 123 feet and 6 inches during his first session and 138 feet and 8 inches during his second session. What is the combined total of the distance walked for the two sessions?
   A) 261 feet 24 inches
   B) 261 feet 6 inches
   C) 262 feet 8 inches
   D) 262 feet 2 inches
   E) 262 feet 4 inches

This is a question on performing a calculation with mixed units. It is usually easiest to perform one calculation with the feet and another with the inches. You may need to convert the total inches back to feet and inches if there are more than 12 inches in the second calculation.

Finding the Best Deal – One-Step Calculations

38) You run a souvenir store that sells key rings. You can get 50 key rings from your first supplier for 50 cents each. You can get the same 50 keys rings from your second supplier for $30 in total, or from your third supplier for $27.50. How much will you pay if you get the best deal?
   A) $25.00
   B) $25.25
   C) $25.50
   D) $27.50
   E) $30.00

This is a question on finding the best deal when you have to perform a one-step calculation. Read the facts carefully, work out the total prices for all three suppliers, and then compare prices.

Finding the Best Deal – Two-Step Calculations

39) A budget hotel charges $45 per night or $280 per week. If you stay at the hotel for 9 nights, what is the least that you will pay for your stay?
   A) $280
   B) $315
   C) $325
   D) $370
   E) $560

This is a question on finding the best deal when you have to perform two-step calculations. Determine the duration of your stay in weeks and nights. Then add the cost for 1 week to the cost for 2 days to solve.

Circles – Area

40) A building project you are designing has a circular tower. The floor of the tower, which has a 12-foot radius, needs to be filled in with concrete. In order to do this, you need to calculate the area of the floor of the tower. What is the approximate area of the floor of the tower in square feet?
   A) 37.68
   B) 75.36
   C) 226.08
   D) 376.80
   E) 452.16

This is a question on calculating the area of a circle. From the formula sheet, we can see that the area of a circle ≈ 3.14 × (*radius*)^2. Substitute the values into the formula and perform the operations to solve.

Circles – Circumference

41) You work as a technician that measures the wear on tractor tires. In order to determine the rate of wear, you must first determine the circumference of each tire. The tire you are currently measuring has a diameter of 46.5 inches. What is the circumference?
   A) 23.500 inches
   B) 73.005 inches
   C) 146.01 inches
   D) 292.02 inches
   E) 1697.4 inches

This is a question on calculating the circumference of a circle. Check your formula sheet for the correct formula to use. Then substitute values and perform the operations to solve.

Rectangles – Area

42) You are making a patchwork quilt that is going to be 6 feet long and 5 feet wide. What will the surface area of the quilt be in square feet?
   A) 11
   B) 22
   C) 25
   D) 26
   E) 30

This is a question on calculating the area of a rectangle. Be sure to use the correct formula from the formula sheet.

Rectangles – Perimeter

43) You need to put up a fence around a field that is 12 yards long and 9 yards wide. What figure below best represents the perimeter of this fence in yards?
   A) 21
   B) 42
   C) 54
   D) 72
   E) 108

This is a question on calculating the perimeter of a rectangle. Remember not to confuse area and perimeter as they are different calculations.

Calculating Discounts

44) The price of an item is normally $15, but customers with a loyalty card can purchase it at the discounted price of $12. What percentage best represents the discount awarded to these customers?
   A) 3%
   B) 5%
   C) 15%
   D) 20%
   E) 25%

This is a question on calculating the percentage of a discount. Divide the dollar amount of the discount by the original price to get the percentage of the discount.

Calculating Markups

45) You own a retail ceramics store that sells mugs and bowls. You buy one type of mug for $3 and sell it for $9. You use the same percentage mark up on one type of bowl that you buy for $4. What figure below represents the sales price of the bowl?
   A) $6
   B) $8
   C) $9
   D) $10
   E) $12

This is a question on calculating a markup. You need to calculate the percentage for the markup on the first product and apply this percentage markup to the second product. Remember to use the percentage markup, rather than a dollar value. You may need the following formulas if you don't already know how to calculate markup: Dollar value of markup = Sales price in dollars – Cost in dollars; Percentage markup = Dollar value of markup ÷ Cost in dollars

Workkeys Practice Test 4 – Level 6

Calculating Reverse Percentages

46) You got $20 off of an order. This amounted to a 25% discount off the order. What would you have paid without the discount?
   A) $4
   B) $5
   C) $25
   D) $60
   E) $80

This is a question on calculating a reverse percentage. To calculate a reverse percentage you need to divide, rather than multiply. So, take the dollar value of the discount and divide by the percentage to solve.

Converting Quantity within Systems of Measurement

47) You are a nutritionist who advises clients and sells supplements to them. A box containing the supplements weighs 8 pounds and 5 ounces when full. The box itself weighs 7 ounces when it is empty. Each supplement weighs 0.75 ounces. About how many supplements should be in the box?
   A) 168
   B) 177
   C) 178
   D) 186
   E) 187

This is a question on performing conversions within systems of measurement. Here we have to convert between pounds and ounces. Convert the total weight of the product (excluding the box weight) to ounces then divide the total ounces by the ounces per unit to solve.

Converting Time within Systems of Measurement

48) You work as a manager for a company that fabricates cleaning products. You begin to make the first batch of products on Monday at 10:30 am. The actual production time is 3 hours and 25 minutes. This is followed by a bottling and labeling process that takes 1 hour and 40 minutes and a packaging process that takes a further 26 hours. If you keep this schedule, when will the first batch be ready for shipment?
   A) Tuesday at 12:30 pm
   B) Tuesday at 3:55 pm
   C) Tuesday at 5:35 pm
   D) Wednesday at 3:55 pm
   E) Wednesday at 5:35 pm

This is a question on calculating the hours and minutes that have passed since the start of a job or process. Calculate the total time for the entire process and add to the starting time to solve.

Identifying Why a Mistake Occurred in a Solution

49) You need to calculate the area of a rectangular object that is 18 inches long and 10 inches wide. You currently have calculated the area as 100 square inches. What mistake did you make in this calculation?
   A) You used the length in the formula where you should have used the width.
   B) You used the width in the formula where you should have used the length.
   C) You should have squared the length, instead of the width.
   D) You should have squared the width, instead of the length.
   E) You should have multiplied the sum of the length and width by 2.

This is a question on identifying the reason for a mistake in a calculation. You may need to perform the steps in each of the answer choices if the reason is not clear to you.

Finding the Best Deal and Performing an Additional Calculation

50) You sell soft drinks in a convenience store that you run. You can buy 240 soft drinks from one supplier for 25 cents each or from a different supplier for $58 for all 240 drinks. Both suppliers are in the same state, so you have to pay a sales tax of 6.5% on either purchase. If you choose the best price for the soft drinks, including tax, how much will you pay in total?
   A) $58.00
   B) $60.00
   C) $61.77
   D) $63.90
   E) $64.50

This is an advanced question on finding the best deal. Remember to add the dollar amount of the sales tax to both calculations for this problem.

Rearranging Formula for the Area of a Circle

51) A circular fish pond that you are designing for your local park has an area of about 78.5 square feet. What is the approximate diameter of the pond?
   A) 5 feet
   B) 10 feet
   C) 15.7 feet
   D) 25 feet
   E) 246.5 feet

This is a question on rearranging a formula. Here, we are given the area of the circle in the facts of the problem, so we have to divide by 3.14, instead of multiplying by 3.14, as stated in the formula. Remember that diameter is double the radius, so if the radius is 3 feet, for example, the diameter is 6 feet.

Rearranging Formula for the Area of a Rectangle

52) You have calculated that you need to plant seeds in a rectangular vegetable garden that has an area of 360 square feet. If the length of the garden is 30 feet, what is the width of the garden?
   A) 12 feet
   B) 24 feet
   C) 115 feet
   D) 150 feet
   E) 330 feet

This is another question on rearranging a formula. From the formula sheet, we know that the area of a rectangle = length × width. Here, we are given the area, so we need to divide that by the length to solve.

Converting Units of Measurement for the Area of a Circle

53) You need to calculate the area of a circular object that has a diameter of 18 feet. However, you need to complete a report that is asking for the area of the object in terms of square inches. Which figure below should you use for your report?
A) 678 square inches
B) 2,289 square inches
C) 3,052 square inches
D) 8,139 square inches
E) 36,625 square inches

This is a question on converting units of measurement. First, we need to calculate the area in terms of square feet. Don't forget to convert your answer further to solve.

Converting Units of Measurement for the Area of a Rectangle

54) You need to calculate the area of the floor of a prison cell for your job as prison administrator. You have determined that the cell is 14 feet long and 9 feet wide. However, you need to convert the area to square yards for record-keeping purposes. What is the area of the prison cell in terms of square yards?
A) 4 square yards
B) 7 square yards
C) 8 square yards
D) 14 square yards
E) 126 square yards

This is another question on converting units of measurement. Calculate the area in terms of square feet, and convert this result further to solve.

Volume of Rectangular Shape

55) You have to fill a tank that holds dye that is used for jeans that your company makes. The tank is 5 feet wide, 8 feet long, and 3 feet high. How many cubic feet of dye can the tank hold when it is completely full?
A) 15
B) 24
C) 40
D) 120
E) 240

Volume of a Cube

56) You need to calculate the amount of polyester filling to place in the footrests that your company manufactures. The footrests are in the shape of a cube that has a side length of 18 inches. How many cubic inches of filling should be placed inside each footrest?
A) 72
B) 81
C) 324

D) 729
E) 5,832

For questions on calculating volume, be sure to use the appropriate formula from the formula sheet. Then substitute values and perform the operations to solve.

Calculating Production Rates by Unit

57) You run a business that makes picture frames for artwork. You can make 20 small frames in 4 days or 21 large frames in 3 days. A customer has just placed an order with you for 40 small frames and 64 large ones. Approximately how many days will it take you to make them all?
   A) 7
   B) 11
   C) 14
   D) 17
   E) 20

This is a question on calculating production rates by unit. Determine the unit rates per day for each of the products by dividing the output by the number of days. Then divide the rates into the amount of items ordered to solve.

Calculating Production Rates by Time

58) You work as a supervisor for a manufacturing company. The report on the current production order shows that 12.5% of the work has been completed in the past 4 days. If work continues at the same rate, how many more days will be required in order to finish the order?
   A) 3
   B) 4
   C) 28
   D) 32
   E) 36

This is a question on calculating rate by time. Calculate the percentage of work completed per day, and then determine how many days are needed for the job.

Identifying Correct Equations to Solve Problems

59) You work in a restaurant that sells different types of sauces with the meals it serves. The sauces come in standardized containers that are labeled with the number of fluid ounces of sauce that each one contains. You need to change the labels so that they show how many cups there are in each container. What formula should you use?
   A) cups = fluid ounces × 8
   B) cups = fluid ounces × 0.125
   C) cups = fluid ounces ÷ 0.08
   D) cups = fluid ounces ÷ 0.125
   E) fluid ounces = cups × 8

This is a question on reworking equations. There are 8 ounces in one cup, so if we had one cup of fluid, we would multiply by 8 to determine the volume in ounces. However, we are given the volume in ounces, so we need to rearrange the formula accordingly.

60) You work as a medical assistant that provides support to clients who are trying to lose weight. The clients are participating in an international trial, so all of the clients' weights are taken in kilograms. However, you need to convert the weights to pounds for use in the United States. Which formula should you use?
A) pounds = kilograms × 2.2
B) pounds = kilograms × 0.0454545
C) pounds = kilograms ÷ 2.2
D) pounds = kilograms + 0.0454545
E) pounds = kilograms × 453.592

This is another question on working out an equation. Notice that this problem is in the section entitled 'Identifying the Correct Equations.'

Workkeys Practice Test 5 – Level 7

Fractions as Quantities

61) You work at a garden store that fertilizes and treats customers' lawns. One customer wants to fertilize and treat his lawn, which is 50¼ feet by 60¼ feet in size. The cost of the fertilizer and treatment is $5.25 per square yard. To the nearest dollar, how much will it cost the customer to fertilize and treat his lawn?
   A) $177
   B) $1,766
   C) $5,298
   D) $15,895
   E) $143,052

> This is a question on working with quantities that contain fractions. Convert the mixed numbers to decimals and multiply. Then perform the conversion to solve.

Fractions as Units

62) You work in a company that manufactures socks. It is company policy to have at least 60 yards of dark black yarn in stock at the start of every month. You have taken inventory this morning and have found that you have 2 balls of dark black yarn that are 75 inches each and 4 balls of dark black yarn that are 25¼ inches each. You must purchase this yarn in 5-yard-long balls. How many balls of yarn do you need to buy in order to replenish your stock?
   A) 10
   B) 11
   C) 33
   D) 36
   E) 39

> This is a question on working with fractional units. Calculate the amount of remaining stock in inches, and then convert from inches to yards. Then calculate the amount required to restock. Remember that it is not possible to buy a fractional part of a ball, so you have to round up to solve.

Decimals as Units

63) You are a machinist who measures the clearance of the closure of doors on washing machines. The current clearance for the door into its aperture is 0.34 millimeter (mm). The clearance should be between 0.22 and 0.28 mm. The clearance is set by using a spacer that reduces the distance between the door and the aperture by the size of the spacer. The spacers come in 0.02 mm increments, and the spacer currently in the machine is 0.16 mm. Which one of the following spacers, in millimeters, should you use in order to have the correct clearance?
   A) 0.02
   B) 0.10
   C) 0.18
   D) 0.22
   E) 0.32

> This is a question on decimal units. The clearance currently measures 0.35 mm with a 0.16 spacer in place, so when the spacer is taken out, the clearance would be 0.16 mm more, so we need to add these two amounts together to get our starting point.

Identifying the Reason for a Mistake

64) You supervise a coating process for one of the types of candy that your company manufactures. The candy coating is prepared in a spherical device that measures 6 feet across on the inside. You have calculated that the inside of the device at its maximum could contain 904.32 cubic feet of coating. What error, if any, did you make in this calculation?
   A) You forgot to use 4/3 from the formula.
   B) You forgot to multiply by 3.14.
   C) You cubed the tank's diameter instead of its radius.
   D) You multiplied the radius by 2, instead of cubing it.
   E) There is no error in your calculation.

This is an advanced question on determining the reason for a mistake. For these types of questions, you will usually have to take time to perform the calculations mentioned in each of the answer choices, but you may be able to eliminate some of the answer choices beforehand if you perform the stated calculation correctly before you try to select your answer.

Converting Units of Measurement – Advanced Problems

65) You work for a company that manufactures liquid cosmetics. You need to test a 0.75-gram sample of an active ingredient of a liquid cosmetic. The correct concentration ratio is 50 milligrams of active ingredient to 1.5 milliliters of liquid. How many milliliters of liquid should you add to the sample?
   A) 0.000015
   B) 0.000225
   C) 12.25
   D) 15.0
   E) 22.5

This is a question on converting grams to milligrams. Use the formula sheet to do the conversion. Then apply the correct ratio to solve.

66) You are responsible for ordering fabric for a company that manufactures T-shirts. You use the costing formula (cost in dollars) = 0.12 × (length in inches) to calculate the cost of royal blue knit fabric. Your manager would like to have the formula in terms of centimeters for the company's international subsidiary. Which one of the following formulas is correct?
   A) (cost in dollars) = 0.00120 × (length in centimeters)
   B) (cost in dollars) = 0.03658 × (length in centimeters)
   C) (cost in dollars) = 0.04724 × (length in centimeters)
   D) (cost in dollars) = 0.30480 × (length in centimeters)
   E) (cost in dollars) = 0.39370 × (length in centimeters)

This is an advanced question on reworking an equation. Your current formula is (cost in dollars) = 0.12 × (length in inches), but you are expressing it in centimeters. So, you would need to multiply the inches by 2.54 to convert the measurement.

It is really important to remember for problems like this one that when you have to multiply the measurement by the conversion factor, you then need to divide the price by the same conversion factor in order to get your new formula to work.

In the same way, when you have to divide the measurement by the conversion factor, you then need to multiply the price by the conversion factor for the new formula.

Determining the Best Deal – Advanced Problems

67) You are trying to find the best deal on some promotional pamphlets that you are going to distribute. You want to print 725 pamphlets and need to find the best deal on getting the pamphlets printed. A printing company in your town charges 20 cents per pamphlet, plus 7% sales tax. An online printing company charges $125 for the whole order plus a $15 delivery charge, but does not charge sales tax. If you choose the best price, how much will you pay for the printing?
A) $140.00
B) $145.00
C) $149.80
D) $155.15
E) $160.15

This is another advanced question on calculating the best deal. Determine the cost for the first supplier plus tax. Then compare to the total cost for the second supplier.

Volume of Spheres

68) Your company processes dairy products. Milk is stored in a spherical storage tank that is 72 inches across on the inside. The tank is now 80% full of milk. What is the volume in gallons of the milk in the tank?
A) 676
B) 846
C) 156,227
D) 195,333
E) 36,097,561

This is a question on calculating volume. Use the appropriate formula and multiply by the percentage stated in the problem. Then do the conversion to solve.

Volume of Cylinders

69) In your work for a wastewater company, you have to determine the volume of water held in certain cylindrical structures. You have been asked to calculate the volume in cubic meters of wastewater in a tank has a 5 meter radius and is 21 meters in height. What figure should you give to your supervisor?
A) 329.7
B) 412.125
C) 549.5
D) 659.4
E) 1648.5

This is another question on calculating volume. Use the appropriate formula, substitute the values, and perform the operations in the formula to solve.

Volume of Cones

70) You work for a confection company that manufactures three different sizes of ice cream cones. The large cones are 6 inches high and have a 1.5 inch radius, the medium cones are 5 inches high and have a 1 inch radius, and the small cones are 4 inches high and have a 0.5 inch radius. You have been asked to calculate the difference between the volume in cubic inches of the large cone and the medium cone. Which figure should you put on your report?
A) 4.19
B) 5.23
C) 8.90
D) 14.13
E) 41.34

This is a question on calculating differences in volumes. Use the appropriate formula to determine the volumes of both cones. Then calculate the difference between the volumes of the two cones to solve.

Rearranging Formulas to Calculate Measurements

71) You are a civil engineer for a company that uses a hammering machine that places rivets into holes in steel joints. You need to specify the diameter of the shaft of the rivet before the work begins. The diameter of each hole is specified as 0.800 inch with a tolerance of ±0.015 inch. The maximum diameter of the shaft of the rivet must be 0.003 inch smaller than the minimum hole diameter. If the diameter of the shaft of the rivet has a tolerance of ±0.0015 inch, what diameter in inches should you specify for the shaft of the rivet?
A) 0.7805
B) 0.7830
C) 0.7850
D) 0.8000
E) 0.8150

This is an advanced question on calculating measurements. Calculate the diameter of the hole, within the tolerance. The diameter of each hole is specified as 0.800 inch with a tolerance of ±0.015 inch. With the tolerance, the diameter of the hole at its maximum could be 0.800 + 0.015 = 0.815, and at its minimum could be 0.800 − 0.015 = 0.785.

Converting Between Units of Measurement – Advanced Problems

72) You are a contractor laying wooden parquet pieces on a floor. The wooden part of the floor will cover an area that measures 8 feet long by 4 feet wide. Each wooden parquet piece measures 12 inches by 6 inches. What is the minimum number of wooden parquet pieces that you will need in order to cover the wooden part of the floor?
A) 16
B) 32
C) 48
D) 64
E) 72

This is another advanced measurement question. Determine how many wooden pieces will fit along the length of the floor. Next, determine how many wooden pieces can fit along the width. Finally, multiply to solve.

Mean

73) An employee receives the following scores on his performance reports during the year: 89, 65, 75, 68, 82, 74, 86. What is the mean of his scores?
A) 24
B) 74
C) 75
D) 77
E) 78

This is a question on calculating the mean. Remember that mean is the same as average. To find the mean, add up all of the items in the set and then divide by the number of items in the set.

Mode

74) Members of a weight loss group report their individual weight loss to the group leader every week. During the week, the following amounts in pounds were reported: 1, 1, 3, 2, 4, 3, 1, 2, and 1. What is the mode of the weight loss for the group?
A) 1 pound
B) 2 pounds
C) 3 pounds
D) 4 pounds
E) 5 pounds

This is a question on mode. The mode is the number that occurs the most frequently in the set.

75) What is the mode of the numbers in the following list? 1.6, 2.9, 4.5, 2.5, 5.1, 5.4
A) 3.5
B) 3.1
C) 3.0
D) 2.5
E) no mode

This is another question on mode. What happens to the mode if no number in the set occurs more than once?

Median

76) The assembly lines in your plant are able to fabricate units at the following rates per minute: 8.19, 7.59, 8.25, 7.35, and 9.10. What is the median of these times?
   A) 7.59
   B) 8.19
   C) 8.25
   D) 8.096
   E) 8.19

This is a question on determining the median. The median is the number that is in the middle of the set when the numbers are in ascending order.

Range

77) Your production team has received the following safety-at-work scores this month: 98.5, 85.5, 80, 97, 93, 92.5, 93, 87, 88, 82. What is the range of these scores?
   A) 17.0
   B) 18.0
   C) 18.5
   D) 89.65
   E) 92.5

This is a question on calculating the range. To calculate the range, the low number in the set is deducted from the high number in the set.

Calculating Mean with a Missing Value

78) There are 10 cars in a parking lot. Nine of the cars are 2, 3, 4, 5, 6, 7, 9, 10, and 12 years old, respectively. If the average age of the 10 cars is 6 years old, how old is the 10th car?
   A) 1 year old
   B) 2 years old
   C) 3 years old
   D) 4 years old
   E) 5 years old

This is a question on how to calculate the missing value from the calculation of the mean. We don't know the age of the 10th car, so set up an equation and put this in as x to solve:
$(2 + 3 + 4 + 5 + 6 + 7 + 9 + 10 + 12 + x) \div 10 = 6$

Mean and Median – Advanced Questions

79) The median and mean of 9 numbers are 8 and 9 respectively. The 9 numbers are positive integers greater than zero. If each of the 9 numbers is increased by 2, which of the following statements must be true of the increased numbers?
A) The mean will be greater than before, but the median will remain the same.
B) The median will be greater than before, but the mean will remain the same.
C) Both the median and mean will be greater than before.
D) The median and mean will be the same as before, but the range will increase.
E) The mean, median, and range will all increase.

If all of the values in a data set are positive integers greater than zero and all of the values increase, the mean and median will also increase, but the range will not change. Conversely, if all of the values in such a data set decrease, the mean and median will also decrease, but the range will not change.

Calculating Mean from Subsets of the Whole

80) 100 participants took an intelligence test. The mean score for the first 50 participants was 82, and the mean score for the next 50 participants was 89. What is the mean test score for all 100 participants?
A) 85.5
B) 86.5
C) 87
D) 88
E) 89

Find the total points for the first group. Then find the total points for the second group. Then divide the total points by the total number of members in the group.

Workkeys Practice Test 6 – Level 3

81) You work for a company that digs wells. The depth of the well is represented as a negative number. The first well you dug this week measured –92 meters, and the second well you dug this week was 120 meters deeper than the first well. What figure below represents the depth of the second well?
A) –120
B) 120
C) –28
D) 212
E) –212

82) You sell kitchen cupboards for a chain store. You get a $350 commission for every set of kitchen cupboards you sell. This week, you sold 11 sets of kitchen cupboards. What is your commission for the week?
A) $350
B) $361
C) $3500
D) $3850
E) $3950

83) Your company sells artwork and prints online. The sales for the first four months of business were: $2516, $3482, $4871, and $5267. What was the total sales for the first four months?
A) $16,082
B) $16,136
C) $16,145
D) $16,181
E) $16,496

84) You run a health club and received $2,496 this month for monthly membership fees. If each member pays the same amount in monthly fees and you have 52 members, what is your monthly membership fee?
A) $4
B) $8
C) $48
D) $52
E) $96

85) You are the cashier in a hardware store. A customer gives you $150 to pay for the items she purchased, which total $127.82. How much change should you give the customer?
A) $22.18
B) $22.27
C) $22.28
D) $22.72
E) $23.28

86) Investment losses are represented as negative numbers, while investment profits are represented as positive numbers. An investor makes the following profits and losses during a six month period: –$1205, $532, $875, –$1359, $1436, and –$982. What was the total investment profit or loss during these six months?
A) $2015
B) $1707
C) $703

D) −$712
　　　E) −$703

87) You have spent ⅛ of the funds allocated to a project. What figure below expresses the amount spent as a decimal number?
　　A) 0.0125
　　B) 0.125
　　C) 12.5
　　D) 0.25
　　E) 2.50

88) You have already sold ⁶/₂₅ of your inventory this month. Approximately what percentage of your inventory have you already sold?
　　A) 0.24%
　　B) 24%
　　C) 2.40%
　　D) 4.167%
　　E) 41.67%

89) 80% of your sales are from sunglasses and other accessories. What fraction best represents this percentage?
　　A) ¾
　　B) ⅗
　　C) ⅘
　　D) 4/6
　　E) ⅚

90) A business reports profit margin, calculated as net income in relation to sales revenue, as a decimal figure. Last year, the profit margin was 0.32. What percentage best represents the profit margin for last year?
　　A) 0.32%
　　B) 3.20%
　　C) 32.0%
　　D) 32.2%
　　E) 320%

91) An eyeglasses store is offering 25% off in a sale this month. What decimal number below best represents the percentage off?
　　A) 0.0025
　　B) 0.2500
　　C) 2.5000
　　D) 25.000
　　E) 250.00

92) You have to package 50 identical items in individual packages. You have completed 0.24 of the entire job. How many items have you packaged so far?
　　A) 6 items
　　B) 12 items
　　C) 18 items
　　D) 24 items
　　E) 38 items

93) You have spent already 0.20 of your monthly budget at the end of the second week of the month. What fraction best represents the amount of the budget you have spent?
   A) 1/8
   B) 1/4
   C) 1/5
   D) 6/8
   E) 5/4

94) You sell candy by the ounce in your convenience store. Customers have to pay 20 cents for each ounce of candy they buy. One customer buys 15½ ounces of candy. How much will he have to pay for this purchase?
   A) $2.10
   B) $3.00
   C) $3.10
   D) $22.50
   E) $25.00

Workkeys Practice Test 7 – Level 4

95) You are a sales order clerk for a large company. Last week, you completed 210 order forms in 35 hours. Assuming that each order form takes the same amount of time to complete, how many minutes should it take you to complete an individual order form?
   A) 0.10 minutes
   B) 1.0 minutes
   C) 10 minutes
   D) 0.6 minutes
   E) 6 minutes

96) A census has revealed that 7 out of every 10 families in a certain city have school-age children living at home. If there are 4,500 families living in this city, how many families with school-age children living at home are in the city?
   A) 643
   B) 700
   C) 1,350
   D) 3,150
   E) 4,500

97) You are a business analyst who calculates the cash flow needs of businesses. Positive cash flow is represented as a positive figure, while negative cash flow is represented as a negative figure. Cash flow figures for a particular business were as follows: Week 1 –$1,503; Week 2 $2,476; Week 3 –$3,087; Week 4 $986. What was the total cash flow for these four weeks?
   A) 1128
   B) –1848
   C) –1155
   D) –1146
   E) –1128

98) A novelty store charges $12 for a certain gift. A customer will need to pay $1.50 more per gift if he or she wants to have it gift wrapped. This month, 51 customers purchased this gift and requested gift wrap. How much money in total did the store make on gifts sold to these 51 customers?
   A) $668.50
   B) $688.50
   C) $612.00
   D) $621.00
   E) $780.30

99) You work for a company that makes stained glass panels for windows. You worked 7 hours on a job each day for 6 days for one customer. The customer was billed $30 per hour for your work, and you were paid $18 per hour. How much money did the company make for your work on these windows after paying your wages?
   A) $108
   B) $126
   C) $504
   D) $756
   E) $1260

100) A company received 132 satisfactory responses from customers on a customer satisfaction questionnaire. 150 customers were questioned for this particular questionnaire. What percentage of the customers' responses was satisfactory?
  A) 0.88%
  B) 8.80%
  C) 82.0%
  D) 88.0%
  E) 79.5%

101) A factory line worker assembles the following number of units over a five-day period. Day 1: 106 units; Day 2: 110 units; Day 3: 108 units; Day 4: 112 units; Day 5: 104 units. On average, how many units did the worker complete per day?
  A) 108
  B) 115
  C) 135
  D) 180
  E) 540

102) You are an independent consultant who undertakes projects for clients. You report the completion status at the end of the week in terms of whole units plus fractional units. This week, you have completed $5^{5}/_{8}$ projects for one client and $3^{3}/_{8}$ projects for another client. What is your total completion status for these two projects at the end of this week?
  A) $2^{1}/_{4}$
  B) 8
  C) $8^{7}/_{8}$
  D) 9
  E) $9^{7}/_{8}$

103) You own a store that creates custom-made curtains and draperies by special order for customers. A customer placed an order, which according to your initial measurements, required $9^{5}/_{12}$ yards of fabric. However, you take the measurements again later and realize that your initial measurement was incorrect. You actually need $10^{7}/_{12}$ yards of fabric for this order. Which amount below represents the change to this order?
  A) $1^{1}/_{6}$ yards more needed
  B) $1^{1}/_{6}$ yards less needed
  C) $1^{1}/_{3}$ yards more needed
  D) $1^{1}/_{3}$ yards less needed
  E) 20 yards now needed in total

104) You manufacture sails for sailboats. You need $25^{7}/_{16}$ yards of sailcloth for one order and $32^{2}/_{16}$ yards of sailcloth for another order. How many yards of sailcloth do you need for both of these orders in total?
  A) $57^{1}/_{4}$
  B) $57^{3}/_{16}$
  C) $57^{9}/_{16}$
  D) $57^{3}/_{4}$
  E) $58^{9}/_{16}$

105) You have to mix herbicide as part of your job as a gardener. The herbicide comes as a liquid that needs to be diluted with water. According to the instructions, you have to add 5 ounces of water for every 2 ounces of herbicide liquid that you use. You are currently making a mixture of the herbicide that should contain 84 ounces of herbicide liquid. How many ounces of water should you add to this mixture?
A) 420
B) 210
C) 84.0
D) 42.0
E) 33.6

106) The human resources department mandates that the ratio of upper-level managers to mid-level managers should be 2:3. So, for every 2 upper-level managers in the company, there should be 3 mid-level managers. If there are 87 mid-level managers, how many upper-level managers are there?
A) 13
B) 29
C) 36
D) 44
E) 58

107) You worked from 9:15 to 9:35 creating 2 hand-made birthday cards. At this rate, how many birthday cards will you make during an 8-hour day?
A) 6
B) 12
C) 36
D) 40
E) 48

108) You need to mix chemicals in a tank to make a sealing treatment for driveways. Your company measures each additive in decimal units, with 100 units representing the filled tank. The tank contains 75.25 units of Chemical X, 10.75 units of Chemical Y, and 3.20 units of Chemical Z. Which of the following represents, in terms of units, how full the tank currently is?
A) 99.2
B) 89.2
C) 88.3
D) 80.2
E) 71.2

109) Your company's online survey results show that 45% of your online reviews are 5-star and 35% of your online reviews are 4-star. What percentage below represents the total amount of online 5-star and 4-star reviews?
A) 80%
B) 70%
C) 45%
D) 35%
E) 10%

110) You have just received an order for 5 holders for tea-light candles. Each tea-light candle holder takes $2\frac{1}{2}$ hours for you to make. How much time is needed to make all five holders?
A) 10 hours and 25 minutes
B) 10 hours and 30 minutes
C) 10 hours and 50 minutes
D) 12 hours and 30 minutes
E) 12 hours and 50 minutes

111) You own a stationery store that sells high quality pens and pencils. After taking inventory this morning, you have determined that you have 350 pens in stock. You want to have 500 pens in stock. You started the month with 105 pens in stock. You purchased 400 pens after the start of the month. You want to determine how many pens you have sold so far this month. Which item below best represents the starting point for solving this problem?
A) number of pens sold last month
B) number of pens in stock
C) number of pens at the beginning of the month
D) number of pens needed to replenish stock
E) the profit made on the sales of the pens

112) You have a contract to paint lines on the highways and county roads for your county. You need to paint lines on 500 miles of roads once every 6 years. You need to paint a double white line down the center of all 500 miles of the roads. On 200 miles of these roads, you also need to paint a single yellow line on the left-side of the road. How many miles of yellow and white lines will you need to paint over the next 12 years?
A) 700
B) 900
C) 1400
D) 2400
E) 2600

Workkeys Practice Test 8 – Level 5

113) You work as a blacksmith that makes iron railings for homes and exteriors. You make your railings in 1/16 inch increments in diameter. You have made a railing that is 5/8 inch diameter, but have realized that it is too large for your current project. What size diameter should you try next?
A) 9/16
B) 11/16
C) 13/16
D) 3/4
E) 3/8

114) You can buy 12 pairs of gloves for $10 in total. Individual pairs of gloves cost $1.50 per pair. What is the best price you will pay if you buy 15 pairs of gloves?
A) $10.00
B) $11.50
C) $13.60
D) $14.50
E) $20.00

115) You perform safety checks on children's car seats and booster seats for your job. You must report the number of units that do not pass the safety inspection each day. A report of your results for the week is shown below. If there is an error in the report, identify the line in which the error appears.

Row	Hour	Units Produced	Passed Inspection	Failed Inspection
1	Monday	980	968	12
2	Tuesday	823	817	6
3	Wednesday	954	942	12
4	Thursday	1026	1018	18
5	Friday	890	879	11

A) Row 2
B) Row 3
C) Row 4
D) Row 5
E) There is no mistake.

116) You own a chain of stores that sell appliances. You can purchase 120 washing machines from your usual supplier for $172 each. You can get the same 120 washing machines from a second supplier for $20,500 in total, or from a third supplier for $19,000 plus 7% sales tax. How much will you pay to get the best deal?
A) $19,000
B) $20,330
C) $20,500
D) $20,640
E) $20,812

117) You make beverages for select retailers. You need 3 quarts and 2 cups of flavoring for your first batch of the day, and 4 quarts and 3 cups of flavoring for your second batch. How much flavoring do you need for both batches in total?
A) 7 quarts and 4 cups
B) 8 quarts and 2 cups
C) 1 gallon and 2 cups
D) 1 gallon and 1 cup
E) 2 gallons and 1 cup

118) You create triangular-shaped corner shelves from oak and other wood for sale to furniture and home stores. You need to report the area of each shelf to the buyer as part of your sales agreement. You need to calculate the area of a triangular-shaped shelf that has a base of 12 inches and a height of 14 inches. What is the area of this shelf in square inches?
A) 56
B) 84
C) 168
D) 1728
E) 2744

119) You need to make a special triangular-shaped corner shelf for a custom order. The customer lives in a 300-year-old house, so the walls are not completely straight and the corners are not completely square. You need to make a triangular shelf that will have one 44° angle and one 47° angle. What is the measurement in degrees of the third angle of this shelf?
A) 45°
B) 45.5°
C) 89°
D) 90°
E) 269°

120) You are painting a wall that is 16 feet long and 11 feet high. You need to calculate the surface area of the wall in order to know how much paint to buy. What is the surface area of the wall in square feet?
A) 54
B) 121
C) 176
D) 256
E) 352

121) As a cartographer, you must calculate the distance between cities in your state. You have measured a distance between two cities of 38 miles. What is the approximate distance between the cities in terms of kilometers?
A) 24
B) 61
C) 125
D) 3800
E) 6100

122) You own a store that sells wallets, purses, and bags. You buy one style of bag for $4 and sell it for $12. You use the same percentage mark up on a second style of bag that you buy for $3. What figure below represents the price of the second style of bag?
A) $9
B) $10
C) $11
D) $12
E) $15

123) You are a real-estate developer who has recently purchased a circular-shaped tower. The first floor of the building has been divided into 5 pie-shaped segments that join at the center of the circle. The first segment measures 82° along the outside edge. The second segment has a measurement of 79°; the third has a measurement of 46° and the fourth has a measurement of 85°. What is the measurement in degrees of outside edge the fifth segment?
A) 48
B) 49
C) 58
D) 68
E) 73

124) You are an electrician who installs wiring in certain household products. The wiring you are installing today is for a refrigerator that has 780 watts and 120 volts. What is the power of the refrigerator in amps?
A) 6.5
B) 65
C) 0.1538
D) 93.6
E) 93,600

125) The price of an item is normally $22.50, but customers with a membership can purchase it at the discounted price of $20. What percentage best represents the membership discount?
A) 0.125%
B) 12.5%
C) 0.111%
D) 11%
E) 25%

Workkeys Practice Test 9 – Level 6

126) You are a school bus driver and are scheduled to depart from school to take children home each day at 3:30 pm. The children live in 10 different homes, which are all stops on your route. You must return the bus back to the school after all of your stops by 5:20 pm. You arrive at the first stop on your route at 3:38 pm, and you have 9 more stops remaining. It takes 17 minutes to drive from your last stop to the school. Average travel time between stops is 6 minutes, and you spend 2 minutes unloading time at each stop. How many minutes will you have to spare when you return the bus back to the school?
  A) 3 minutes
  B) 13 minutes
  C) 21 minutes
  D) 29 minutes
  E) 30 minutes

127) You sell toys in a toy store that you own. You can buy 350 units of a particular type of toy from one supplier for 85 cents each or from a different supplier for $295 for all 350 units. You will have to pay a sales tax of 8.5% on either purchase. If you choose the best price for the toys, including tax, how much will you pay in total?
  A) $295.00
  B) $297.50
  C) $320.08
  D) $320.29
  E) $322.79

128) You need to calculate the volume of medicine in a beaker for your job as a lab technician. The beaker is cylindrical and measures 18 inches high and 12 inches in diameter. However, you have to convert the volume from cubic inches to gallons for a report you need to complete. What is the approximate volume of the beaker in terms of gallons?
  A) 2.9 gallons
  B) 8.8 gallons
  C) 10.4 gallons
  D) 8,138.88 gallons
  E) 470,200 gallons

129) You have received $123 off an order. This amounted to a 40% discount off the original price. How much would you have paid without the discount?
  A) $30.75
  B) $49.20
  C) $205.00
  D) $307.50
  E) $492.00

130) You run a company that supplies food products to caterers in your area. You can buy tomato sauce by the crate. A crate containing 100 cans of tomato sauce weighs 90 pounds and 12 ounces. The crate weighs 15 pounds when it is empty. Each can of tomato sauce weighs 12 ounces. Approximately how many cans of tomato sauce are in the crate?
  A) 101
  B) 121
  C) 139
  D) 1200
  E) 1212

131) You need to calculate the circumference of a circular object that has a 12-inch radius. You have erroneously calculated the circumference as 452 inches. What mistake did you make in this calculation?
A) You used the formula for circular area instead of the formula for circumference.
B) You should have squared the radius, instead of just using the radius.
C) You should have used the diameter, instead of the radius.
D) You should have multiplied by the radius, instead of the diameter.
E) You have forgotten to multiply by 3.14.

132) You need to fill a rectangular solid container with a liquid substance. The length of the rectangular solid is 12 feet, the width is 9 feet, and the volume is 1080 cubic feet. What is the height of the rectangular solid?
A) 10 feet
B) 12 feet
C) 90 feet
D) 100 feet
E) 120 feet

133) You work for a company that sells different types of rope. The rope comes in coiled bundles that are labeled with the number of feet in each bundle. You need to change the labels so that they show the length of each one in millimeters. What formula should you use?
A) millimeters = feet × 0.3048
B) millimeters = feet × 0.3048 × 1,000
C) millimeters = feet ÷ 0.3048
D) millimeters = feet × 0.3048 ÷ 1,000
E) millimeters = feet ÷ 0.3048 ÷ 1,000

134) You work as a land surveyor who measures farmland for the county deeds office. The surveying equipment you use reports the result in terms of square yards. However, you need to convert the measurements to acres for the report you have to prepare. Which formula should you use?
A) acres = (square yards × 9) ÷ 43,560
B) acres = (square yards × 9) × 43,560
C) acres = (square yards ÷ 9) ÷ 43,560
D) acres = (square yards ÷ 9) × 43,560
E) acres = square yards × 43,560

135) You need to calculate the volume of a cube-shaped object that has a side length of 9 feet. However, you need to complete a report that is asking for the volume of the object in terms of cubic inches. Which figure below should you use for your report?
A) 729 cubic inches
B) 1,259 cubic inches
C) 1,728 cubic inches
D) 139,968 cubic inches
E) 1,259,712 cubic inches

136) You work for a lumber yard and have to take measurements of various products in board feet. You have an order of lumber that measures 14 inches by 12 inches by 12 inches. What is the volume of this order in terms of board feet?
A) 14 board feet
B) 144 board feet
C) 168 board feet
D) 2,016 board feet
E) 20,160 board feet

137) You work as an engineer for an electricity company. You have discovered that the majority of your company's customers use 32,000 watt-hours of electricity per day. You need to report this amount in terms of kilowatt hours (kWh) for your report. How many kilowatt-hours of electricity do the majority of your customers use per day?
A) 3.2 kWh
B) 32 kWh
C) 320 kWh
D) 32,000 kWh
E) 32,000,000 kWh

138) You work as a climatologist and need to calculate the average high temperature in one city over a five-day period in degrees Celsius. However, the high temperatures are reported in Fahrenheit. You have collected the following data: Day 1: 72° F; Day 2: 68° F; Day 3: 65° F; Day 4: 82° F; Day 5: 81° F. What was the approximate average high temperature in degrees Celsius?
A) 74°C
B) 73°C
C) 41°C
D) 32°C
E) 23°C

139) You own a hairdressing salon that provides haircuts, styling, and other services to customers. Your manicurist has reported that it takes 5 hours to do 4 full manicures and 2.5 hours to do 5 full pedicures. How long should it take your manicurist to do 20 full manicures and 25 full pedicures?
A) 7 hours and 30 minutes
B) 12 hours and 30 minutes
C) 25 hours
D) 37 hours and 30 minutes
E) 37 hours and 50 minutes

140) You work as a librarian for a local community college. A recent report on a publishing project shows that shows that 57.75% of the project has been completed in the past 7 work days. If work continues at the same rate, approximately how many work days will be required in total for the entire project?
A) 9
B) 10
C) 12
D) 14
E) 21

Workkeys Practice Test 10 – Level 7

141) You are trying to find the best deal on some veterinary supplies for your veterinary practice. You want to purchase 135 units of a certain feline medication. One company charges $15.30 per unit, plus 6% sales tax. Another company charges $2,100 for the whole order plus a $75 administration charge, but does not charge sales tax. If you choose the best price, how much will you pay for the medication?
   A) $2,065.50
   B) $2,100.00
   C) $2,175.00
   D) $2,189.43
   E) $2,305.50

142) Your company ships products overseas in large rectangular shipping containers. One type of container is 25 feet long, 12 feet wide, and 18 feet high. The container is currently 75% full of a particular product. What is the volume in cubic yards of the product in the container?
   A) 150 cubic yards
   B) 200 cubic yards
   C) 405 cubic yards
   D) 4,050 cubic yards
   E) 109,350 cubic yards

143) You work for a company that manufactures glue and other adhesives that contain a chemical called PVA. You need to have at least 50 quarts of PVA in stock at the start of every month. You have taken inventory this morning and have found that you have 2 containers of PVA that hold 16 cups and 7 ounces each. You also have 3 containers of PVA that hold 20 cups and 4 ounces each. You must purchase this PVA in 5-quart containers. How many containers do you need to buy in order to replenish your stock?
   A) 0
   B) 5
   C) 6
   D) 7
   E) 27

144) You are a machinist who measures the clearance for valves into their chambers. The current clearance for the valve into its chamber is 0.46 millimeter (mm). The clearance should be between 0.31 and 0.34 mm. The clearance is set by using a spacing device that reduces the distance between the valve and the chamber by the size set on the spacer. The spacer settings are in 0.03 mm increments, and the spacer setting currently in use in the chamber is 0.12 mm. Which one of the following spacer settings, in millimeters, should you use in order to have the correct clearance?
   A) 0.03
   B) 0.12
   C) 0.24
   D) 0.30
   E) 0.36

145) You work for a company that manufactures hand soap and laundry detergent. Each month, you have to order liquid parabens that are used in your products. The parabens are stored in two identically sized vats. The vats measure 10 feet by 10 feet by 12 feet. The first vat is $3/4$ full and the second vat is $4/5$ full. The parabens cost 12 cents a cubic inch. To the nearest dollar, what is the cost value of the parabens in the two vats?
   A) $223
   B) $3,857

C) $4,977
D) $385,690
E) $497,664

146) Your company manufactures batteries, and you supervise the process for filling the batteries with acid. The acid is stored in a conical-shaped container that is 6 feet in diameter and 8 feet in height. You have calculated that the inside of the container at its maximum could contain approximately 226 cubic feet of acid. What error, if any, did you make in this calculation?
A) There is no error in your calculation.
B) You forgot to multiply by 3.14.
C) You squared the container's diameter instead of its radius.
D) You multiplied the radius by 2, instead of squaring it.
E) You forgot to divide by 3.

147) You are responsible for purchasing the active ingredient for a foot-care product. You use the costing formula (cost in cents) = 0.18 × (volume in gallons) to calculate the cost of the product. Your manager would like to have the formula in terms of liters for the company's international division. Which one of the following formulas is correct?
A) (cost in cents) = 0.0475 × (volume in liters)
B) (cost in cents) = 0.0682 × (volume in liters)
C) (cost in cents) = 0.4752 × (volume in liters)
D) (cost in cents) = 0.6818 × (volume in liters)
E) (cost in cents) = 0.6818 ÷ (volume in liters)

148) You work for a company that manufactures wooden sheds. You ship lumber from an overseas supplier at a rate of $3.65 per board foot. Your current shipment of lumber is 26 feet by 14 feet by 10 feet. What will you pay your supplier for the lumber in this shipment?
A) $92
B) $159,432
C) $1,594,320
D) $1,913,184
E) $22,958,208

149) You received the following scores from a customer satisfaction survey: 9.8; 8.7; 9.5; 7.9; 8.6; 6.3; 9.9; 5.4. What is the mean of your scores?
A) 8.2625
B) 8.65
C) 9.4
D) 66.10
E) 98.4875

150) You own a fuel oil company. You have sold the following amounts of fuel oil in gallons to customers this week: 325, 420, 175, 275, 385, 475, 325, 180, 435, 505. What is the mode in gallons?
A) 175
B) 275
C) 325
D) 330
E) 350

151) You have had the following amounts of expenditure each month for the first six months of the year: January: $342; February: $712; March: $634; April: $958; May: $534; June: $869. What is the mode expenditure?
A) no mode
B) 616
C) 637
D) 673
E) 675

152) You have manufactured the following amounts of product during a 7-day period: 104, 103, 98, 102, 96, 100, 105. What is the median amount?
A) 101.1
B) 101.5
C) 102.0
D) 102.5
E) 141.6

153) You are an electrician who installs wiring and lighting in new homes. The client would like you to install lights on the walls in the living room. The living room is 25 feet long and 10 feet wide. The client would like a light to be installed on each wall in 5-foot increments. However, no lights are to be installed in the corners of the room. How many lights will you need to carry out this job?
A) 8
B) 10
C) 12
D) 14
E) 16

154) You work for a company that makes ice cubes and frozen refreshments. Your company makes two sizes of ice cubes. The large ice cubes have a side length of 1.8 millimeters, and the small ice cubes have a side length of 1.4 millimeters. What is the amount in cubic millimeters of the difference in volume between the large ice cube and the small one?
A) 0.064
B) 1.960
C) 2.744
D) 3.088
E) 5.832

155) You have been asked to calculate the areas of two triangular shapes in your job as a building engineer. The large triangle has a base of 12 inches and a height of 18 inches. The small triangle has a base of 8 inches and a height of 14 inches. What is the difference in the areas of the two shapes?
A) 8
B) 16
C) 25
D) 52
E) 56

Workkeys Practice Test 11 – Mixed Level

156) You sell magazine subscriptions online. You get $59 upfront per customer for every customer who signs up during the week. This week, 14 customers signed up. How much did you make on upfront subscription fees for these customers this week?
   A) $726
   B) $762
   C) $826
   D) $862
   E) $926

157) You have $3/8$ of your inventory left at the end of this financial quarter. How much inventory do you have left when expressed as a decimal number?
   A) 0.0375
   B) 0.375
   C) 3.750
   D) 0.125
   E) 12.50

158) You need to calculate the changes to the weight of packaging for your products. When packaging weigh has decreased, it is represented as a negative number. When packaging weight has increased, it is represented as a positive number. Packaging weight changes for your first three years of business were as follows. Year 1: –92 grams; Year 2: 35 grams; Year 3: –16 grams. What figure below represents the change in the packaging weight from year 1 to year 2?
   A) –57
   B) 57
   C) 19
   D) 127
   E) –127

159) Your expenses for your first three years of business were: $12,225; $43,871; and $69,423. What were the total expenses for your first three years of business?
   A) $125,339
   B) $125,465
   C) $125,519
   D) $125,528
   E) $130,019

160) A customer gives you $75 to pay for the items she purchased, and you gave her the correct change of $8.35. What was the total cost of the items she purchased?
   A) $66.65
   B) $66.75
   C) $65.65
   D) $66.55
   E) $65.55

161) You have invested in some stock options, which can go up or down in value each day. Investment gains are represented as positive numbers, and investment losses are represented as negative numbers. You have invested in five different companies, and at the end of one particular day, your gains and losses were as follows: –205, 39, –107, 18, 126. What was your total investment gain for loss for all five investments for this day?
   A) 85
   B) 129

C) −129
D) −192
E) −381

162) You work for an auto shop that does custom paint and vinyl wrap jobs on vintage cars. You worked 7.5 hours each day for 2 days on a job for one customer. The customer was billed $75 per hour for your work, and you were paid $40 per hour. How much money did the shop make for your work on this job after paying your wages?
A) $262.50
B) $300.00
C) $525.00
D) $600.00
E) $1125.00

163) You have a liquid ingredient that you store in 5-quart containers. You have two partially-full containers, one with $4^3/_8$ quarts and another with $3^7/_8$ quarts. How many quarts do you have in total in these two containers?
A) $1^1/_4$
B) 7
C) $7^1/_8$
D) $8^1/_4$
E) $9^1/_4$

164) You own a small factory that uses tarpaulin to make covers for farm implements. According to your measurements, you started the day with $12^7/_{16}$ yards of tarpaulin. When you take measurements again at the end of the day, you have $8^9/_{16}$ yards of tarpaulin left. Which amount below represents the amount of tarpaulin used this day in yards?
A) $2^{14}/_{16}$
B) $3^1/_8$
C) $3^7/_8$
D) $4^7/_8$
E) 21

165) You have purchased 80 items for sale and have sold 0.75 of them in relation to the total purchased. How many items do you have left after making these sales?
A) 10 items
B) 20 items
C) 25 items
D) 40 items
E) 60 items

166) You are a market researcher and need to keep records on teenage consumer habits. A local school has agreed to let you collect data from one of their classes. You are collecting data from a class which has n students. In this class, $t\%$ of the students subscribe to digital TV packages. Which of the following represents the number of students who do not subscribe to any digital TV package?
A) $100(n - t)$
B) $(100\% - t\%) \times n$
C) $(100\% - t\%) \div n$
D) $(1 - t)n$
E) $(n - t)$

167) You own a shop that sells sugar-craft products. For a particular product, you must add 3 parts of icing sugar for every 6 parts of sugar paste. You need to prepare a batch of sugar-craft that has 14 parts of sugar paste. How many parts of icing sugar should you add to this batch?
A) 3
B) 6
C) 7
D) 8
E) 9

168) You are a quality-control supervisor for a company that manufactures electronics. You have just checked a shipment of 100 mp3 players. In this shipment, 1% of the mp3 players are faulty. What is the ratio of non-faulty mp3 players to faulty mp3 players?
A) 1:100
B) 100:1
C) 99:100
D) 1:99
E) 99:1

169) You own a store that sells cells phones and accessories. You purchase a certain brand of cell phone at a cost of x and sell the cell phones at four times the cost. Which of the following represents the markup on each of these cell phones?
A) x
B) $3x$
C) $4x$
D) $3 - x$
E) $3 + x$

170) You are an internet provider that sells internet packages based on monthly rates. The price (P) for the internet service depends on the speed (s) of the internet connection. The chart that follows indicates the prices of the various internet packages.
Price in Dollars: $10 $20 $30 $40
Speed in GB: 2   4   6   8
Which equation represents the prices of these internet packages?
A) $P = (s - 5) \times 5$
B) $P = (s + 5) \times 5$
C) $P = 5 \div s$
D) $P = s \times 5$
E) $P = s \times 1/5$

171) You have started a production schedule for a new product. In the first few days of production, output will be low as new problems are encountered and solved. During the first nine hours of production, the following amounts of units were produced per hour: 1, 2, 3, 4, 5, 5, 8, 8, 9. Which figure below represents the mean production in units per hour for the first nine hours of production?
A) 1
B) 2
C) 5
D) 8
E) 9

172) You are responsible for data entry for orders for a small manufacturing company. You received seven orders yesterday for the following numbers of units: 12, 20, 3, 25, 30, 28, and 18. What was the median number of units ordered yesterday?
A) 12
B) 13
C) 20
D) 35
E) 30

173) Your company sells jeans and T-shirts. J represents jeans and T represents T-shirts in these equations: 2J + T = $50 and J + 2T = $40. A customer buys one pair of jeans and one T-shirt. How much does she pay for her entire purchase?
A) $10
B) $20
C) $30
D) $40
E) $70

174) You manufacture galvanized pipe in 1/64 inch increments in diameter. You have selected a pipe that is 23/64 inch diameter, but have realized that it is too large for your current work order. What size diameter should you select next?
A) 1/4
B) 11/32
C) 12/32
D) 13/32
E) 1/8

175) You own a chain of stores that sells footwear. You can purchase 325 pairs of tennis shoes from your normal supplier for $4 a pair. You can get the same 325 pairs of shoes from a second supplier for $1,250 plus 6% sales tax, or from a third supplier for $1,290. How much will you pay to get the best deal?
A) $1,250.00
B) $1,290.00
C) $1,300.00
D) $1,367.40
E) $1,378.00

176) You are an HVAC engineer for heating, ventilation, and air-conditioning units that are sold in Europe. All European HVAC appliances and systems must be 220 volts to conform to European Union law. You are designing an air-conditioning system for the European market. Your specifications state that the system should have an output of 35 amps. What should the specification in watts be for this air-conditioning system?
A) 4.15
B) 6.29
C) 62.9
D) 7,700
E) 11,660

177) You can buy cotton cloth for your textile manufacturing company for $3 a meter from an overseas supplier. However, you need to report the cost of the cloth in inches for your financial statements for the board of directors. How many inches of cloth can you get for $3?
A) 2.54
B) 3.937
C) 39.37

D) 100
E) 254

178) You work as an architect for a firm in your city. You often have to calculate length and angles for the drawings you prepare for clients. You are preparing a drawing that contains a triangle. The triangle has one angle, labeled Angle A, which measures 36°. You are missing the measurements for angles B and C of this triangle. However, you have noted that angles B and C have the same measurement each in degrees. What is the measurement of angle B?
A) 36°
B) 45°
C) 72°
D) 144°
E) Cannot be determined from the information provided.

179) You own a gardening store that sells sod, turf, and artificial grass. A customer has requested a quote for artificial grass for a football field. In order to calculate the price to quote to the customer, you need to calculate the area of the football field. The customer has informed you that the football field is 100 yards long and 30 yards wide. What is the area of the football field in square yards?
A) 130
B) 150
C) 300
D) 1500
E) 3000

180) You own a farm and have several fields in which your livestock grazes. You need to order barbed wire for a small pasture that has a length of 5 yards and a width of 3 yards. The barbed wire must be long enough to be placed on all four sides of the outside of this pasture. How many yards of barbed wire should you order?
A) 15
B) 16
C) 18
D) 40
E) 52

181) You make ornamental embellishments for benches for parks and lawns. You are making a circular ornament that has a diameter of 12. Before you continue fabricating the ornament, you need to calculate its circumference. Which equation should you use?
A) 6 × 3.14
B) 12 × 3.14
C) 24 × 3.14
D) 36 × 3.14
E) 144 × 3.14

182) You work for a company that manufactures boxes and other packaging products. A particular box is manufactured to contain either laptop computers or notebook computers. When the computer systems are removed from the box, it is reused to hold other items. If the length of the box is 20 centimeters (cm), the width is 15cm, and the height is 25cm, what is the volume of the box in cubic centimeters?
A) 150
B) 300
C) 750
D) 7500
E) 15,000

183) You supervise a fast-paced, mechanized production line for a well-known retail item. The production line has 6 different production stages that the item must pass through before it is completed. Each production stage lasts for 9 seconds, and the set-up time for each stage is an additional 2 seconds. The production line shift begins at 6:00 AM and a count of items produced takes place every 10 minutes, with the first count to take place at 6:10 AM. The items are counted after they are placed into a box, and there is a further 5 second packaging time for each box that is filled. How many items will you have packaged in the box when you take your first count at 6:10 AM?
A) 0
B) 6
C) 9
D) 37
E) 54

184) You work for a factory that manufactures tires and customized rims for high-end collectible cars. Once the tire is mounted onto the rim, the weight of each tire-and-rim product is 32 pounds and 4 ounces. The product is loaded into a wooden crate, and the crate when empty weighs 60 pounds. Each individual rim weighs 19 pounds. The crate when completely full to capacity weighs 447 pounds. How many units can each crate contain?
A) 11
B) 12
C) 13
D) 14
E) 16

185) You work for the county surveyor's office and have to calculate the distance between various landmarks in your area in kilometers for overseas reporting purposes. However, the distances in the report also need to be converted to feet for comparison to United States urban planning statistics. Which formula should you use to convert kilometers to feet?
A) feet = (kilometers × 0.62) ÷ 5,280
B) feet = (kilometers × 0.62) × 5,280
C) feet = (kilometers ÷ 0.62) × 5,280
D feet = (kilometers ÷ 0.62) ÷ 5,280
E) kilometers = (feet × 0.62) × 5,280

186) You have to interpret distances on maps and perform distance conversions for your examination as a civil engineer. The legend for the map states that 1 inch on the map is equal to 20 miles in actual distance. There is a space of 2 and a half inches between two cities on the map. What figure below best represents the actual distance in kilometers between these two cities?
A) 31.06
B) 32.2
C) 80.5
D) 322
E) 805

187) You have an online sales business, and you need to package and ship your product in boxes to your customers each day. You can package 5 boxes in 1 and a half hours. You need 4 extra minutes per box to fill out a shipping form in order to prepare the box for shipment. You need to package 14 boxes and prepare them for shipment today. How long should it take you to package all 14 boxes and prepare them for shipment?
A) 2 hours and 52 minutes
B) 4 hours and 12 minutes
C) 5 hours and 8 minutes
D) 3 hours and 8 minutes
E) 4 hours and 16 minutes

188) You work in a store that sells tropical fish and treatments for aquariums. A certain brand of aquarium water treatment comes in a 2-quart size container. You repackage this into two sizes of bottles for resale. You sell an 8-ounce size bottle of the treatment and a larger 12-ounce size bottle. You have checked your inventory, and you have 3 quarts of the treatment left in stock. You want to be able to have 25 units of the 8-ounce bottles and 20 units of the 12-ounce bottles on the shelf for sale and a further 4 quarts left in stock after you have filled all of the bottles. How many containers of the treatment do you need to buy in order to fill all of the bottles and have 4 quarts left in stock?
A) 8
B) 14
C) 15
D) 16
E) 18

189) Your company manufactures glassware, and you are responsible for ordering high-grade sand for use in the glass-making process. The sand is stored in a rectangular container that is 9 feet high, 6 feet long, and 5 feet wide. You have been asked to calculate the volume of the container in cubic yards. You have calculated that the volume of the container is 270 cubic yards. What error, if any, did you make in this calculation?
A) There is no error in your calculation.
B) You forgot to divide by 27 to convert cubic feet to cubic yards.
C) You forgot to multiply by 27 to convert cubic feet to cubic yards.
D) You calculated the perimeter instead of the area.
E) You forgot to multiply by 1,728.

Workkeys Practice Test 12 – Mixed Level

190) You own an art and craft store, and this year you collected $7,375 for sales of a certain type of scrapbook. If you sell these scrapbooks for $59 each, how many of them did you sell this year?
A) 135
B) 125
C) 120
D) 75
E) 59

191) You have to measure the depth of substances in petri dishes for your job. Some of the substances may expand due to bacterial growth, and some of the substances may decrease, in which case the result will be represented as a negative number. You measured the results for five dishes this week and have recorded the following figures: 52, –14, 37, –28, 61? What was the total growth or decrease for all five dishes?
A) –108
B) 60
C) 78
D) 108
E) 133

192) You have already sold $6/25$ of your inventory this month. Approximately what percentage of your inventory have you already sold?
A) 0.24%
B) 2.40%
C) 24.0%
D) 4.167%
E) 41.67%

193) Your membership subscriptions have increased 25% this year. What fraction best represents this percentage?
A) $1/4$
B) $1/25$
C) $3/4$
D) $2/5$
E) $1/5$

194) You report changes to monthly cash flow as a decimal figure, which is calculated by dividing the net change in cash flow into the previous month's cash flow. Last month, the change to cash flow was 0.40. What percentage best represents the change to cash flow for last month?
A) 0.40%
B) 4.00%
C) 40.0%
D) 400%
E) 4000%

195) The temperature on Saturday was 62°F at 5:00 PM and 38°F at 11:00 PM. If the temperature fell at a constant rate on Saturday, what was the temperature at 9:00 PM?
A) 58°F
B) 54°F
C) 50°F
D) 46°F
E) 40°F

196) You run a diner that sells hot and cold food. Hot dogs sell for $2.50 each, and hamburgers sell for $4 each. You have just received an order ticket from one of your wait staff. However, the ticket has not been filled out correctly. You know that the customers at this table bought 3 hamburgers. They also bought hot dogs. The total of their ticket was $22. How many hot dogs did they buy?
A) 2
B) 3
C) 4
D) 5
E) 6

197) You own a painting and interior decorating business. You need to paint 8 rooms, each of which has a surface area of 2000 square feet. If one bucket of paint covers 900 square feet, what is the fewest number of buckets of paint that must be purchased to complete all 8 rooms?
A) 3
B) 17
C) 18
D) 19
E) 20

198) You are conducting a study of the jogging and walking speeds of participants of various ages. One participant named Soon Li jogged 3.6 miles in 3/4 of an hour. What was her average jogging speed in miles per hour?
A) 2.7
B) 4.0
C) 4.2
D) 4.6
E) 4.8

199) You run the bookstore at the local technical college. You occasionally offer sales and reductions on certain publications. The price of a certain book is reduced from $60 to $45 at the end of the semester. By what percent is the price of the book reduced?
A) 15%
B) 20%
C) 25%
D) 33%
E) 45%

200) You work for the department of education in your state. As part of your job, you need to calculate statistics on classes in schools in the state. You are currently compiling a report for Carson Heights High School. The ratio of males to females in the senior year class of Carson Heights High School was 6 to 7. If the total number of students in the class was 117, how many males were in the class?
A) 48
B) 54
C) 56
D) 58
E) 63

201) You are a group leader of a weight loss group in your town. Members of the weight loss group report their individual weight loss to you every week. During the week, the following amounts in pounds were reported: 1, 1, 3, 2, 4, 3, 1, 2, and 1. What is the mean of the weight loss for the group?
A) 1 pound
B) 2 pounds
C) 3 pounds

D) 4 pounds
E) 18 pounds

202) You work for the social services department. You need to calculate the average ages of children in the families you assist. One particular family has 5 children. However, your data for this family is incomplete. The ages of 5 siblings are: 2, 5, 7, 12, and x. If the mean age of the 5 siblings is 8 years old, what is the age (x) of the 5th sibling?
A) 8
B) 10
C) 12
D) 14
E) 16

203) You are a work-motion consultant who helps companies evaluate productivity and work practices. You are conducting a work-motion study this week. Work-motion scores for one employee for each day of the week were as follows: 8.19, 7.59, 8.25, 7.35, and 9.10. What is the median of this employee's scores?
A) 7.59
B) 8.19
C) 8.25
D) 8.096
E) 40.48

204) You own a restaurant that offers special prices on take-out orders. The total price paid for a take-out order depends on the quantity of food purchased. This week, you are running a special on chicken sandwiches. The table below shows the relationship between the total number of chicken sandwiches a customer can buy and the total price for each order. If a customer takes the deal that has the lowest price per sandwich, what will the customer pay per sandwich?
2 chicken sandwiches for $17.50
4 chicken sandwiches for $34.40
8 chicken sandwiches for $68.00
A) $4.00
B) $8.00
C) $8.50
D) $9.50
E) $10.00

205) You run a small pizzeria that sells three different types of pizza. You sold 15 cheese pizzas, 10 pepperoni pizzas, and 5 vegetable pizzas one day. Cheese pizzas sell for $10 each; pepperoni pizzas sell for $12, and the total sales of all three types of pizza for that day was $310. What price did you charge per vegetable pizza?
A) $5
B) $8
C) $9
D) $10
E) $12

206) You work as a marketing consultant for a zoo. The zoo has reptiles, birds, quadrupeds, and fish. At the start of the year, they have a total of 1,500 creatures living in the zoo. The percentages by category for the 1,500 creatures at the start of the year were as follows: Reptiles 42%; Quadrupeds 26%; Birds 17%; Fish 15%. At the end of the year, the zoo still has 1,500 creatures, but reptiles constitute 40%, birds 23%, and quadrupeds 21%. How many more fish were there at the end of the year than at the beginning of the year?
A) 10
B) 11

C) 15
D) 16
E) 150

207) Shanika works as a car salesperson. She earns $1,000 a month in basic pay, plus $390 for each car she sells. If she wants to earn at least $4,000 this month, what is the minimum number of cars that she must sell this month?
A) 6
B) 7
C) 8
D) 9
E) 10

208) In your job as an air-traffic controller, you need to plot in 20-minute intervals the speed of each airplane that you are monitoring. One private airplane flew at a constant speed, traveling 780 miles in 2 hours. How many miles did this plane travel in the last 40 minutes of its journey?
A) 120
B) 180
C) 200
D) 260
E) 380

209) You train racehorses for national racing events. Your best horse just ran 12 furlongs in 2 minutes and 48 seconds. Assuming that the same amount of time was spent on each furlong, how many seconds does it take your horse to run one furlong?
A) 0.014 seconds
B) 0.14 seconds
C) 1.40 seconds
D) 14 seconds
E) 168 seconds

210) A national report states that 30 out of every 100 television viewers watch TV for more than 25 hours her week. If there are 3,200 television viewers in your town, how many television viewers in your town watch TV for more than 25 hours per week?
A) 320
B) 750
C) 960
D) 1,067
E) 2,500

211) You sell a particular item on a well-known online shopping website. You charge $22 for the item if the customer collects it in person from your premises, or you charge an extra $3 for postage and handling if the customer wants the item sent by courier. This week, 32 customers purchased this item and requested that the item be sent by courier. How much money in total did you make on the items sold to these 32 customers?
A) $96
B) $575
C) $608
D) $704
E) $800

212) You manufacture duct tape from a special adhesive plastic. The adhesive plastic comes in linear yards. You need 107³/₈ yards of adhesive plastic to complete one work order and 96¹/₈ yards of adhesive plastic for another work order. How many yards of adhesive plastic do you need in total in order to complete both of these work orders?
A) 193¹/₈
B) 203¹/₂
C) 193¹/₄
D) 203¹/₄
E) 213¹/₂

213) You mix colorant in a vat as part of a process of making custom rugs. A single rug can use combinations of up to four different colorants in order to achieve a desired shade. You measure each colorant in decimal units, with the vat holding a maximum of 450 units when it is completely full. The vat contains 163.75 units of red colorant, 107.50 units of blue colorant, 91.25 units of yellow colorant, and 10.30 units of black colorant. Which of the following represents, in terms of units, how full the vat is after these 4 colorants have been placed in it?
A) 362.50
B) 371.50
C) 372.80
D) 373.50
E) 373.80

214) You own a sewing and notions store that sells high quality lace for bridal gowns and bridesmaids' dresses. You need to order materials for 6 bridesmaids' dresses, each of which requires 7 yards of Swiss lace. You have 40 yards of Swiss lace on hand when you start making the dresses, and you would like to have 15 yards of Swiss lace on hand once you have finished making all 6 dresses. You started the month with 10 yards of Swiss lace on hand. You purchased 50 yards of lace after the start of the month. You want to determine how much lace will be left on hand after selling the lace for these 6 dresses. Which item below best represents the first calculation you will need to perform before you start making this order?
A) the amount of lace needed for all 6 dresses
B) the amount of lace you would like on hand
C) the amount of lace at the end of the month
D) number of lace needed to replenish stock
E) the profit made on the sales of the Swiss lace for the 5 dresses

215) You are going to begin making 5 quilts for a customer who owns a small hotel. Each quilt requires 2 yards of red fabric for the front, 1 yard of blue fabric for the front, and a further 3 yards of blue fabric for the back. The quilts need to have an embellishment in gold, and a total amount of 6 yards of gold fabric is needed to make the embellishments for all 5 quilts. Each quilt also has edging in white, and half a yard of white material is needed for the edging for each quilt. The customer calls just as you are to start making the quilts, and requests that the order be doubled. How many yards of fabric in total will you need to complete this order?
A) 7.7
B) 77
C) 3.85
D) 38.5
E) 62

216) You have a field in which cows graze. You are going to buy fence panels to put up a fence along one side of the field. Each panel is 8 feet 6 inches long. You need 11 panels to cover the entire side of the field. How long is the field?
A) 60 feet 6 inches
B) 72 feet 8 inches
C) 93 feet 6 inches
D) 102 feet 8 inches
E) 110 feet 6 inches

217) You tile floors and walls with ceramic tiles. The area of a square floor that you are going to tile is 64 square units. You need to cover the floor entirely with tiles. Each floor tile is 4 square units. How many tiles are needed to cover the floor?
A) 8
B) 12
C) 16
D) 24
E) 32

218) The base of a cylinder is at a right angle to its sides. The radius of the base of the cylinder measures 5 centimeters. The height of the cylinder is 10 centimeters. What is the volume of this container in cubic centimeters?
A) 785
B) 157
C) 78.5
D) 31.4
E) 15.7

219) Cone A has a base radius of 9 and a height of 18. Cone B has a base radius of 3 and a height of 6. Which number below expresses the ratio of the volume of Cone A to Cone B?
A) 27
B) $1/27$
C) 3
D) $1/6$
E) 9

220) In your job as a statistician, you must evaluate the results of market research and product development surveys for statistical validity. You need to prepare a report which breaks down responses into the categories of 'disallowed' or 'valid' when the results of the survey have been compiled. A report of your results for the most recent survey is shown below. If there is an error in the report, identify the line in which the error appears.

Line	Region	Surveys Received	Disallowed Responses	Valid Responses
1	North	1,072	31	1,041
2	East	1,257	59	1,198
3	South	946	49	897
4	West	1,325	51	1,274

A) Line 1
B) Line 2
C) Line 3
D) Line 4
E) There is no mistake.

221) You can purchase 500 units of a particular item of your inventory for 72 cents each from one supplier or from a different supplier for $350 for all 500 units. You will have to pay a sales tax of 5.5% on either purchase. If you choose the best price for the items, including tax, how much will you pay in total?
A) $350.00
B) $360.00
C) $369.25
D) $379.80
E) $542.50

222) As an administrative assistant for a bariatric surgeon, you receive reports from South America that have obesity statistics in terms of kilograms per capita by city. You need to convert these statistics to ounces per capita. Which formula should you use?
A) ounces = (kilograms × 1,000) ÷ 28.53
B) ounces = (kilograms × 1,000) × 28.53
C) ounces = (kilograms ÷ 1,000) × 28.53
D) ounces = (kilograms ÷ 1,000) ÷ 28.53
E) kilograms = (ounces × 1,000) ÷ 28.53

223) You are an engineer who calculates measurements for the clearance for pistons into their cylinders. For the engine you are currently working on, the clearance should be between 0.03 and 0.06 cm. The measurement of the diameter of the piston is currently 12.6 cm. The diameter of the cylinder is 12 cm. The clearance is set by using a device that reduces the diameter of the piston in 0.03 cm increments. Before you use the device to reduce the size of this piston, the device is set to 0.18 cm. By which of the following amounts in increments should you increase the setting on the device in order to have the correct clearance?
A) 2
B) 20
C) 16
D) 17
E) 21

Workkeys Practice Test 13 – Mixed Level

224) A recent survey shows that 42% of your clients would like to receive additional services. What decimal number represents this percentage?
   A) 0.0042
   B) 0.0420
   C) 0.4200
   D) 42.000
   E) 420.00

225) You strive to have 0.20 of your inventory in stock at the end of each month. What fraction represents this decimal number?
   A) 1/8
   B) 1/4
   C) 1/5
   D) 2/5
   E) 4/5

226) You own a store that sells domestic cleaning products. You sell a certain type of liquid cleaner in increments of 1/4 of a cup. Each 1/4 of a cup costs 50 cents. One customer buys $10\frac{1}{4}$ cups of this cleaner. How much will she pay for this purchase?
   A) $5.13
   B) $5.50
   C) $10.50
   D) $20.50
   E) $205.00

227) A customer gives you $160 to pay for the items she purchased, and you gave her the correct change of $12.64. What was the total cost of the items she purchased?
   A) $147.36
   B) $143.76
   C) $137.36
   D) $133.76
   E) $93.36

228) Your cost of sales figures each month for your first five months of business this year were: $723, $618, $576, $812, and $984. What was the total cost of sales for your first five months of business this year?
   A) $743
   B) $3,623
   C) $3,713
   D) $3,722
   E) $3,893

229) You have spent $2/5$ of your operating budget at the end of 6 months of doing business. How much of your operating budget have you spent when expressed as a decimal number?
   A) 0.20
   B) 0.40
   C) 0.45
   D) 2.50
   E) 4.00

230) Your human resources department has informed you that 4 out of every 5 employee-satisfaction questionnaires have been completed and returned. If your company has 250 total employees, and every employee must complete and return the questionnaire, how many questionnaires have not been completed and returned?
A) 4
B) 5
C) 50
D) 200
E) 246

231) You sell poinsettia plants for $20 during December and for $12 during January. In December, 55 customers purchased poinsettias, and 20 customers purchased them in January. How much money did you receive for poinsettia sales during December and January?
A) $240
B) $1,060
C) $1,100
D) $1,340
E) $1,500

232) You work as a flight attendant for a major airline. During each flight, you are required to count the number of passengers on board the aircraft. The morning flight had 52 passengers more than the evening flight, and there were 540 passengers in total on the two flights that day. How many passengers were there on the evening flight?
A) 244
B) 296
C) 488
D) 540
E) 592

233) You run a cafeteria that serves spaghetti to senior citizens on Fridays. The spaghetti comes prepared in large containers, and each container holds 15 servings of spaghetti. The cafeteria is expecting 82 senior citizens this Friday. What is the least number of containers of spaghetti that the cafeteria will need in order to serve all 82 people?
A) 4
B) 5
C) 6
D) 7
E) 15

234) You are an entomologist who observes various insects and their behavior. This week you are studying the movement and speed of a certain type of caterpillar. The caterpillar travels 10.5 inches in 45 seconds. How far will it travel in 6 minutes?
A) 45 inches
B) 63 inches
C) 64 inches
D) 84 inches
E) 90 inches

235) You are an administrative assistant for a sales enterprise. Each week, you need to tabulate the results of customer satisfaction surveys by region and evaluate the bonuses paid. This week, you are tabulating the survey results for four regions, each of which has one salesperson. Salespeople in each region receive bonuses based on the amount of positive customer feedback they receive. The results of the surveys were as follows:
Region 1: 40 positive customer feedback results
Region 2: 30 positive customer feedback results
Region 3: 20 positive customer feedback results
Region 4: 30 positive customer feedback results
If the four salespeople received $540 in bonuses in total, how much bonus money does your company pay each individual salesperson per satisfied customer?
A) $4.00
B) $4.50
C) $4.90
D) $5.00
E) $5.40

236) Return on investment (ROI) percentages are provided for seven companies. The ROI will be negative if the company operated at a loss, but the ROI will be a positive value if the company operated at a profit. The ROI's for the seven companies were: –2%, 5%, 7.5%, 14%, 17%, 1.3%, –3%. Which figure below best approximates the mean ROI for the seven companies?
A) 2%
B) 5.7%
C) 6.25%
D) 7.5%
E) 20%

237) A plumber charges $100 per job, plus $25 per hour worked. He is going to do 5 jobs this month. He will earn a total of $4,000. How many hours will he work this month?
A) 10
B) 40
C) 80
D) 140
E) 160

238) As part of your job as a museum administrator, you need to report the number of visitors to the museum each day of the week. The number of visitors the museum had on Tuesday (T) was twice as much as the number of visitors it had on Monday (M). The number of visitors it had on Wednesday (W) was 20% greater than that on Tuesday. Which equation can be used to calculate the total number of visitors to the museum for the three days?
A) W + .20W + 2T + M
B) 2M + T + W
C) M + 1.2T + W
D) M + 2T + W
E) 5.4M

239) The students at Lyndon High School have been asked about their plans to attend the Homecoming Dance. The chart below shows the responses of each grade level by percentages. Which figure below best approximates the percentage of the total number of students from all four grades who will attend the dance? Note that each grade level has roughly the same number of students.

	Will Attend	Will Not Attend	Undecided
Freshmen:	45%	24%	31%
Sophomores:	30%	45%	25%
Juniors:	38%	20%	42%
Seniors:	30%	25%	45%

A) 25%
B) 35%
C) 45%
D) 55%
E) 60%

240) You run an employment agency for temporary employees. You charge your client $15 per hour for each hour the temporary employee works, you pay the temporary employee $12 an hour, and you retain the difference as a commission. You had 10 employees who worked 40 hours each this week. How much did you make on commission for these 10 employees this week?
A) $30.00
B) $120.00
C) $1,200.00
D) $4,800.00
E) $6,000.00

241) 49 out of the 50 items in your product line had above average sales this month. What percentage of the items in your product line had above average sales this month?
A) 0.098%
B) 0.98%
C) 9.80%
D) 98%
E) 980%

242) Your sales each day for the past five days have been as follows: $90, $85, $85, $105, $110. What was the daily average sales amount during this five-day period?
A) $25
B) $85
C) $90
D) $95
E) $97

243) You own a fabric store and sell ribbon in 3-inch or one-foot increments. One customer wanted two types of ribbon, and you sold her $8^{3}/_{4}$ feet of one type of ribbon and $7^{1}/_{2}$ feet of another type. How much ribbon did this customer buy in total?
A) 7 feet and 6 inches
B) 8 feet and 9 inches
C) 15 feet and 3 inches
D) 16 feet and 3 inches
E) 16 feet and 6 inches

244) You own a business that prepares work orders to a strict time-budget system. Hours spent on a work order are recorded by the tenth of an hour in 6 minute increments. For a particular work order, $28^{3}/_{10}$ hours in total have been budgeted. You have already spent $7^{9}/_{10}$ hours on the work order. Which amount below represents the amount of time left for this work order?
A) $36^{1}/_{5}$
B) $35^{6}/_{10}$
C) $20^{2}/_{5}$
D) $20^{3}/_{5}$
E) $21^{6}/_{10}$

245) In your job in a quarry, you need to mix different kinds of decorative stone for customers to use for landscaping. For one type of decorative stone mix, you have to put in 2 parts of white gravel for every 3 parts of blue slate chippings. You have an order that requires 147 parts of blue slate chippings. How many parts of white gravel should you add?
A) 73.5
B) 88.0
C) 98.0
D) 220.5
E) 294.0

246) You manufacture absorbent disposable products that consist of a single layer of absorbent cotton wadding on the inside and a double layer polyvinyl carbonate sheeting on the outside. Each layer of absorbent cotton wadding is 18 inches long, and each layer of polyvinyl carbonate sheeting is 19 inches long. You need to make 18 of these products for a single order. How many feet of materials in total will be required to manufacture this order?
A) 55.5
B) 56
C) 84
D) 666
E) 1,008

247) You can buy a case containing 24 bottles of motor oil for $50 a case wholesale. Individual bottles of this brand of motor oil cost $2.50 per bottle wholesale. What is the best price you will pay if you buy 100 bottles of motor oil wholesale?
A) $200.00
B) $200.10
C) $202.50
D) $210.00
E) $250.00

248) You make flavored rice cakes for sale worldwide. Units sold in the United States are measured in ounces, and units sold overseas are measured in grams. You need 39 ounces of flavoring for a batch of rice cakes for the United States and 1,190.7 grams of the same flavoring for another batch of rice cakes to sell overseas. How much flavoring do you need for both batches in total?
A) 43.38 grams
B) 2,297.35 grams
C) 40.48 ounces
D) 71 ounces
E) 81 ounces

249) You need to order lightweight ceiling tiles to install a suspended ceiling for a customer whose ceiling is 25 feet wide and 35 feet long. The customer would like you to use a particular type of square ceiling tile that measures 6 inches by 6 inches. How many of these square ceiling tiles do you need to install this ceiling?
A) 438
B) 480
C) 875
D) 1,750
E) 3,500

250) As a nurse practitioner in a busy hospital, you need to dispense a particular medication in milligrams to individual patients in your unit. However, you need to fill out your report for the month in grams. For this month, you dispensed 1,275,000 milligrams of medication to patients. How many grams should you report?
A) 127.5
B) 1,275
C) 12,750
D) 127,500,000
E) 1,275,000,000

251) You work for a company that manufactures sporting goods, and you have to determine the volumes of the inflatable products in the company's product range, You have been asked to calculate the volumetric capacity of a basketball that has a diameter of 10 inches. However, you need to report the volume in cubic centimeters for your European division. Which figure below best represents the volumetric capacity of the basketball in cubic centimeters?
A) 32
B) 523
C) 4,824
D) 8,576
E) 68,607

252) You purchase cell phone covers for resale and sell them in your kiosk in the mall for a retail price of $12 per unit. This amounts to a 525% markup over your cost for each unit. How much does each unit cost you?
A) $0.192
B) $1.92
C) $6.25
D) $0.75
E) $7.50

253) You need to convert the temperature from degrees Fahrenheit to degrees Celsius. You were trying to convert 85° Fahrenheit, and your conversion calculation was 94.64° Celsius. What mistake, if any, did you make in doing this conversion?
A) You divided by 0.56 instead of multiplying by 0.56.
B) You added 32 instead of subtracting 32.
C) You multiplied by 1.8 instead of dividing by 1.8.
D) You divided by 1.8 instead of multiplying by 1.8.
E) There is no mistake.

254) The perimeter of a rectangle is 350 feet and the width of the shortest side is 75 feet. What is the measurement of the length of the rectangle?
A) 10 feet
B) 90 feet
C) 95 feet
D) 100 feet
E) 110 feet

255) You work for a company that manufactures breakfast cereals and cake mixes. You have to place an order for the rice flour which is used in one of your products. The rice flour is stored in three identically sized boxes. The boxes measure 3 feet by 3 feet by 2 feet each. The first box is $1/6$ full, the second box is $1/2$ full, and the third box is $2/3$ full. You want to replenish your supply of rice flour so that you have three full boxes. The rice flour costs 9 cents a cubic inch. To the nearest dollar, what will it cost to replenish the stock in the three boxes?
A) $270
B) $466
C) $998
D) $4,666
E) $7,465

256) You are responsible for ordering leather for the purses and bags that your company makes. You use the formula (cost in dollars) = 0.535 × (length in inches) to calculate the cost of one type of leather used in your products. You need to have the formula in terms of centimeters for the company's international division. Which one of the following formulas should you provide to them?
A) (cost in dollars) = 0.2106 × (length in centimeters)
B) (cost in dollars) = 0.2106 ÷ (length in centimeters)
C) (cost in dollars) = 1.3589 × (length in centimeters)
D) (cost in dollars) = 1.3589 ÷ (length in centimeters)
E) (cost in dollars) = 0.1631 × (length in centimeters)

Workkeys Practice Test 14 – Mixed Level

257) You need to measure the changes to the moisture content inside homes and offices for your job as a building inspector. When there is evaporation and moisture has decreased, the result is represented as a negative number. When moisture has increased due to condensation, it is represented as a positive number. Moisture changes inside a particular structure over 4 weeks were as follows. Week 1: −14 milligrams; Week 2: 15 milligrams; Week 3: −12 milligrams: Week 4: −5 milligrams. What figure below represents the change in the moisture content of this structure from week 3 to week 4?
   A) −17
   B) −7
   C) 7
   D) −16
   E) 16

258) You sell cleaning products door to door. You get $1,250 basic pay per month plus a $12 commission every time a customer orders more than $100 worth of products. This month, you had 32 customers who ordered more than $100 worth of products. How much have you earned in total this month?
   A) $866
   B) $1262
   C) $1634
   D) $1643
   E) $2274

259) You own a farm store, and you carry a certain type of insecticide for sale. This month, you received $310 for the sales of this type of insecticide. If you sell this insecticide for $12.40 each, how many of them did you sell this month?
   A) 6
   B) 25
   C) 38
   D) 52
   E) 3844

260) Your overhead expenses have decreased 10% this year. What fraction best represents this percentage?
   A) $1/10$
   B) $1/4$
   C) $9/10$
   D) $1/100$
   E) $1/5$

261) You run a small store that sells fruit and vegetables. Oranges always sell better than apples, so you like to keep the ratio of bags of apples to bags of oranges at 2 to 3. If there are 44 bags of apples in your store now, how many bags of oranges are there?
   A) 33
   B) 48
   C) 55
   D) 63
   E) 66

262) A dance academy had 300 students at the beginning of January. It lost 5% of its students during the month. However, 15 new students joined the academy on the last day of the month. If this pattern continues for the next two months, how many students will there be at the academy at the end of March?
A) 285
B) 300
C) 310
D) 315
E) 320

263) You own a store that sells ladies' clothing and accessories. The price of a wool coat is reduced 12.5% at the end of the winter. If the original price of the coat was $120, what will the price be after the reduction?
A) $108.00
B) $107.50
C) $105.70
D) $105.00
E) $100.00

264) You work as a quality inspector for a factory that makes microchips. The factory produces 20 times as many functioning chips as defective chips. If the factory produced 11,235 chips in total last week, how many of them were defective?
A) 535
B) 561
C) 1,070
D) 10,700
E) 11,215

265) Your town has recently suffered a flood. The total cost, represented by variable C, which is available to accommodate R number of residents in emergency housing is represented by the equation C = $750R + $2,550. If the town has a total of $55,000 available for emergency housing, what is the greatest number of residents that it can house?
A) 68
B) 69
C) 70
D) 71
E) 75

266) As part of your job with the state department of energy, you need to keep statistics on energy usage by private users. The data on kilowatt-hours of usage per day for one private user was as follows: 2.5, 9.4, 3.1, 1.7, 3.2, 8.2, 4.5, 6.4, 7.8. What was the median value of kilowatt usage for this customer?
A) 3.2
B) 4.5
C) 5.2
D) 6.4
E) 7.7

267) You monitor employee performance in your job as a manager for a manufacturing company. A new employee was able to produce the following number of units each hour that he worked: 89, 65, 75, 68, 82, 74, and 86. What is the mean of the number of units that he produced per hour?
A) 24
B) 74
C) 75

D) 77
E) 82

268) As part of your business in preowned-car sales, you keep track of the ages of the cars that you sell. There are currently 8 cars in your parking lot. 7 of the cars are 2, 3, 4, 5, 9, 10, and 12 years old, respectively. If the average age of the 8 cars is 6 years old, how old is the 8th car?
A) 8 years old
B) 6 years old
C) 5 years old
D) 4 years old
E) 3 years old

269) You record the number of traffic violations that occur every week in your city for your job as a city clerk. The fine for speeding violations is $50 per violation. The fine for other violations is $20 per violation. This week, there were 60 speeding violations, 30 parking violations, and 90 other violations. The total collected for all three types of violations was $6,000. What is the fine for each parking violation?
A) $20
B) $30
C) $40
D) $100
E) $140

270) The price of a sofa at your furniture store was x dollars on Wednesday this week. On Thursday, you reduced the price of the sofa by 10% of Wednesday's price. On Friday, you reduced the price of the sofa again by 15% of Thursday's price. Which of the following expressions can be used to calculate the price of the sofa on Friday?
A) $(0.25)\,x$
B) $(0.75)\,x$
C) $(0.10)(0.15)\,x$
D) $(0.10)(0.85)\,x$
E) $(0.90)(0.85)\,x$

271) You own a clothing store that sells jackets and jeans at a discount during your sales period. T represents the number of jackets sold and N represents the number of jeans sold. The total amount of money the store collected for sales of jeans and jackets during the sales period was $4,000. The amount of money earned from selling jackets was one-third of that earned from selling jeans. The jeans sold for $20 a pair. How many pairs of jeans did the store sell during the sales period?
A) 15
B) 20
C) 150
D) 200
E) 3000

272) Statistics indicate that 81% of the residents of your town are satisfied with the services they receive from city hall. What decimal number represents this percentage?
A) 0.00081
B) 0.00810
C) 0.08100
D) 0.81000
E) 81.0000

273) You calculate your sales discount as a decimal number, instead of a percentage. You offer a discount of 0.35 off the original prices in January every year. What fraction represents this decimal number?
A) 1/35
B) 10/35
C) 7/20
D) 9/20
E) 2/5

274) You had two projects to complete for one particular client this month. You spent $37^{2}/_{5}$ hours on the first project and $25^{4}/_{5}$ hours on the other project. How many hours have you spent on projects for this client this month?
A) $63^{1}/_{5}$
B) $62^{1}/_{5}$
C) $53^{1}/_{5}$
D) $52^{1}/_{5}$
E) $11^{3}/_{5}$

275) Research indicates that the best customer to sales-clerk ratio for high-end luxury stores is 3 to 1. A particular store is expecting 15 customers tomorrow. How many sales clerks should it have available?
A) 1
B) 3
C) 5
D) 12
E) 35

276) It took you from 9:15 AM to 10:25 AM to paint 7 square yards. You have to paint 17.5 square yards in total for this particular job. If you continue at the same pace, what time will you finish painting?
A) 11:10 AM
B) 11:10 PM
C) 11:30 AM
D) 12:10 PM
E) 12:10 AM

277) You need to combine 1235.35 units of product A, 567.55 units of product B, and 347.25 units of product C for the order you are currently processing. Which of the following represents the total number of units for all of the products in this order?
A) 914.80
B) 1582.60
C) 1802.90
D) 2149.15
E) 2150.15

278) You own a small store that sells magazines and dispenses soft drinks. You buy your soft drink in 20 gallon containers. You have one container with $19^{3}/_{4}$ gallons and another with $14^{3}/_{4}$ gallons of soft drink. How much soft drink do you have in total in these two containers?
A) 5
B) $33^{1}/_{2}$
C) $33^{3}/_{4}$
D) $34^{1}/_{2}$
E) $34^{3}/_{4}$

279) You own a company that manufactures aluminum products. You started the month with $102^{7}/_{18}$ yards of aluminum sheeting and have $24^{11}/_{18}$ yards of aluminum sheeting left at the end of the month. Which figure below represents the amount of aluminum sheeting used this month in yards?
A) $77^{7}/_{9}$
B) $78^{7}/_{9}$
C) $77^{2}/_{9}$
D) $78^{2}/_{9}$
E) $79^{7}/_{9}$

280) You work in a hospital unit that has 14 patients. It takes you $1^{3}/_{4}$ hours in total to prepare medications and treatments when you arrive at work every morning. You spend 15 minutes doing files and administrative work for each patient on your unit per day. You work an 8-hour daily shift. How much time do you have left to devote to other tasks each day after you prepare medications and treatments and finish your files and administrative work?
A) 2 hours and 5 minutes
B) 2 hours and 15 minutes
C) 2 hours and 45 minutes
D) 3 hours and 30 minutes
E) 5 hours and 15 minutes

281) Six of your members of staff have received scores on their annual performance reviews as follows: 96, 89, 63, 98, 81, 77. What was the average annual performance review score for these 6 employees?
A) 73.5
B) 79.5
C) 82.5
D) 84.0
E) 85.5

282) The radius (R) of circle A is 5 centimeters. The radius of circle B is 3 centimeters. Which of the following statements is true?
A) The difference between the areas of the circles is approximately 6.28.
B) The difference between the areas of the circles is approximately 28.26.
C) The difference between the circumferences of the circles is approximately 6.28.
D) The difference between the circumferences of the circles is approximately 12.56.
E) The difference between the circumferences of the circles is approximately 18.84.

283) You work as a tire engineer for a pneumatic factory and need to keep statistics about the life and wear of the products that your company sells. A large tire (L) has a radius of 10 inches. A smaller tire (S) has a radius of 6 inches. If the large tire is going to travel 360 revolutions, approximately how many more revolutions does the small tire need to make to cover the same distance?
A) 120
B) 240
C) 360
D) 600
E) 620

284) A rectangle has a length of 18 inches and a width of 10 inches. What is the perimeter of the rectangle in inches?
A) 36
B) 46
C) 56
D) 180
E) 1800

285) You need to make a hard-wearing partition to divide the floor space of a circular arena. The circumference of the floor space of the arena is approximately 1,017.36 feet. Your partition needs to be placed in the middle of the floor space in order to create two equal semi-circular parts. What is the measurement in yards of the partition?
A) 6
B) 18
C) 108
D) 180
E) 324

286) You can purchase Product A from your supplier for $20 per unit. With your membership card, you can get a $4 discount per unit on Product A from the supplier. Your supplier has started to offer the same percentage discount on Product B. You can normally purchase Product B for $16 per unit. What figure below represents the purchase cost of Product B after the discount?
A) $3.20
B) $4.00
C) $12.00
D) $12.80
E) $16.00

287) You need to calculate the volume of a rectangular-shaped container that has a side length of 10 inches, a height of 7 inches, and a width of 5 inches. However, you need to complete a report that is asking for the volume of the container in terms of gallons. Which figure below best approximates the volume of the container in gallons?
A) 80,850
B) 350
C) 152
D) 15.2
E) 1.52

288) You take meter readings for your job with a utilities company. The average meter reading is 1,200 kilowatt hours per month. What is the average in terms of watt hours per month?
A) 1.2
B) 120
C) 120,000
D) 1,200,000
E) 12,000,000

289) You own an automotive supply store. You need to buy 210 units of a particular car accessory. You can get the product for $3.25 a unit from Supplier A plus 5% sales tax. Supplier B will charge you $695 for all 210 units, plus a $25 order fulfillment fee, but does not charge sales tax. If you choose the best price, how much will you pay for all 210 products?
A) $682.50
B) $695.00
C) $716.63

D) $720.00
E) $776.16

290) You have to mix a liquid product for patients as part of your job as a herbal therapy practitioner. The herbal therapy product comes as a liquid that needs to be diluted with organic wheat grass juice. To get the correct concentration, you have to add 3 ounces of herbal therapy product to every 2 cups of organic wheat grass juice that you use. You are currently making a mixture that contains 14 cups of organic wheat grass juice. How many ounces of herbal therapy product should you add to the juice to get the correct concentration for this batch of product?
A) 6
B) 7
C) 11
D) 21
E) 42

291) You travel on a delivery route that has rest points marked out at equal intervals. There are 7 rest points on the route, including the rest point at your final destination. It takes $1\frac{1}{4}$ hours to travel to the first rest point. You are allowed a maximum 15 minute break at each rest point. If you travel at a constant speed, how much on-the-road time is needed, excluding time resting, in order to travel to your final destination?
A) 7 hours and 15 minutes
B) 7 hours and 45 minutes
C) 8 hours and 45 minutes
D) 10 hours
E) 10 hours and 30 minutes

Workkeys Practice Test 15 – Mixed Level

292) You are calculating gains or setbacks in productivity in your company. Some production lines may increase in their productivity, which will be represented as a positive number, and some production lines may experience setbacks, in which case the result will be represented as a negative number. You measured the gains and setbacks for your company's four production lines and have recorded the following figures: −14, 52, −36, −7. What was the total gain or setback for all four production lines?
A) −23
B) 23
C) 9
D) −5
E) 5

293) You have already achieved 9/16 of your projected sales for this year. Approximately what percentage of your projected sales have you already achieved?
A) 0.5625%
B) 5.625%
C) 56.25%
D) 43.75%
E) 0.04375%

294) Your employee retention rate is calculated by dividing the number of employees who work for your company at the end of the year into the number of employees who worked for your company at the start of the year. Last year, the employee retention rate was 0.95. What percentage best represents the employee retention rate for last year?
A) 0.95%
B) 9.50%
C) 95.0%
D) 950%
E) 9500%

295) Your employee loss rate is calculated by dividing the number of employees who left your company during the year into the total number of employees in your company at the start of the year. You had 120 employees at the start of the year, and your employee loss rate was 0.05 for the year. How many employees do you have at the end of the year?
A) 5
B) 6
C) 12
D) 104
E) 114

296) You own a furniture store that sells tables, chairs, and other types of furniture. You have given a 20 percent discount this month on one of the tables that you sell. This amounts to a discount of $60. What was the original price of the table?
A) $80
B) $120
C) $1200
D) $300
E) $3000

297) You order 10-quart containers of ice cream for the ice cream business that you own. You started the day on Wednesday with 6³/₄ quarts of praline nut ice. At the close of business that Wednesday, you had 2¹/₂ quarts of praline nut ice cream left. How much praline nut ice cream did you sell that day?
A) 4¹/₄
B) 4³/₈
C) 4⁵/₈
D) 4⁶/₈
E) 5¹/₄

298) You work in a factory that manufactures pesticides. You need to use 9 ounces of liquid for every 6 ounces of active chemical that you use. Your current job lot requires 10 ounces of active chemical. How many ounces of liquid should you add?
A) 1.50
B) 15.0
C) 0.67
D) 67.0
E) 150

299) Susan wanted to find the mean of the six surveys she administered this month. However, she erroneously divided the total points from the six surveys by 5, which gave her a result of 96. What is the correct mean of her six surveys?
A) 63
B) 80
C) 82
D) 91
E) 92

300) You make brownies, cakes, and other confections daily for your own store. You allow your employees to take home the goods that you have not sold by the close of business each day. You have 3 partial trays of unsold brownies at the end of the day, and each tray has ¹/₈ of the brownies left in it. You need to divide these remaining brownies among four employees. What amount below represents the fraction of a tray of brownies that each employee will receive?
A) ¹/₆
B) ³²/₃
C) ³/₂₄
D) ⁴/₂₄
E) ³/₃₂

301) You are a medical assistant in a clinic for patients trying to lose weight. This month Person A lost 14³/₄ pounds, Person B lost 20¹/₅ pounds, and Person C lost 36.35 pounds. What is the total weight loss for this group of patients?
A) 70.475
B) 71.05
C) 71.15
D) 71.25
E) 71.30

302) You purchased 50 reams of paper to use in your office this month. At the end of the month, you have used 5 of these reams of paper. Which decimal figure below best expresses the amount of reams of paper that you have used in relation to the amount of reams that you purchased?
A) 0.0010
B) 0.0100
C) 0.1000

D) 0.0500
E) 0.5000

303) You screen and interview prospective employees in your job in human resources. One hundred prospective candidates took an aptitude test for a new job opening. The 55 female candidates had an average score of 87, while the 45 male candidates had an average of 80. What was the average aptitude test score for all 100 candidates?
A) 82.00
B) 83.15
C) 83.50
D) 83.85
E) 84.00

304) Mary works for a charity and needs to get $650 in donations. So far, she has obtained 80% of the money she needs. How much money does she still need?
A) $8.19
B) $13.00
C) $32.50
D) $81.85
E) $130.00

305) The Abdul family is shopping at a superstore that you own. They buy product A and product B. Product A costs $5 each, and product B costs $8 each. They buy 4 of product A. They also buy a certain quantity of product B. The total value of their purchase is $60. How many units of product B did they buy?
A) 4
B) 5
C) 6
D) 8
E) 15

306) You sell socks and shoes in the shoe store that you run. The price of socks is $2 per pair and the price of shoes is $25 per pair. Anna went shopping for socks and shoes, and she paid $85 in total. In this purchase, she bought 3 pairs of shoes. How many pairs of socks did she buy?
A) 2
B) 3
C) 5
D) 8
E) 15

307) You sell chain-link fence by the 1/2 yard. You sell each 1/2 yard for $10.50. One customer buys $20^{1}/_{2}$ yards of this particular type of fence. How much will the customer pay for this purchase?
A) $215.25
B) $225.75
C) $430.50
D) $450.50
E) $451.50

308) You need $49^{3}/_{16}$ inches of rope of to finish one job and $18^{1}/_{16}$ inches to finish another. How many inches of rope do you need in order to complete both jobs?
A) $66^{1}/_{8}$
B) $67^{1}/_{8}$
C) $66^{1}/_{4}$

D) 67¼
E) 67¾

309) You conduct quality control for a factory that makes computer chips. On your most recent shift, you were surprised to discover that 11 out of 132 chips were defective. What percentage best represents the amount of defective computer chips in relation to the total?
A) 0.08%
B) 8%
C) 83%
D) 92%
E) 83%

310) You own a company that manufactures specialty bread, biscuits, and cakes. When making soda-bread biscuits, the best proportion of baking soda to flour is 2 to 9. You are making a batch of soda-bread biscuits that calls for 126 cups of flour. How many cups of baking soda should you use?
A) 6
B) 7
C) 14
D) 18
E) 28

311) You worked from 12:10 PM to 2:25 PM knitting 3 caps by hand from alpaca yarn. At this rate, how many caps will you knit during a 9-hour period?
A) 6
B) 12
C) 36
D) 27
E) 48

312) Your company manufactures a weight-loss product. Your market research shows that 58% of your customers are 10 to 20 pounds overweight and 27% of your customers are 21 to 30 pounds overweight. What percentage below represents the amount of customers that are 10 to 30 pounds overweight?
A) 27%
B) 31%
C) 75%
D) 85%
E) 95%

313) If a circle has a radius of 4, what equation can be used to calculate the circumference of the circle?
A) 3.14 ÷ 8
B) 3.14 ÷ 16
C) 8 × 3.14
D) 16 × 3.14
E) 36 × 3.14

314) If a circle has a radius of 6, what equation can be used to calculate the area of the circle?
A) 6 × 3.14
B) 12 × 3.14
C) 24 × 3.14
D) 36 × 3.14
E) 3.14 ÷ 36

315) If circle A has a radius of 0.4 and circle B has a radius of 0.2, what is the difference in area between the two circles?
   A) 0.1256
   B) 0.3768
   C) 0.5024
   D) 1.256
   E) 1.884

316) A rectangular box has a base that is 5 inches wide and 6 inches long. The height of the box is 10 inches. What is the volume of the box in cubic inches?
   A) 30
   B) 110
   C) 150
   D) 300
   E) 3000

317) Find the area of the right triangle whose base is 2 and height is 5.
   A) 2.5
   B) 5
   C) 10
   D) 15
   E) 22.5

318) Find the approximate volume of a cone which has a radius of 3 and a height of 4.
   A) 12.56
   B) 37.68
   C) 4.1762
   D) 2.355
   E) 50.24

319) Pat wants to put wooden trim around the floor of her family room. Each piece of wood is 1 foot in length. The room is rectangular and is 12 feet long and 10 feet wide. How many pieces of wood does Pat need for the entire perimeter of the room?
   A) 22
   B) 44
   C) 100
   D) 120
   E) 144

320) The Johnson's have decided to remodel their upstairs. They currently have 4 rooms upstairs that measure 10 feet by 10 feet each. When they remodel, they will make one large room that will be 20 feet by 10 feet and two small rooms that will each be 10 feet by 8 feet. The remaining space is to be allocated to a new bathroom. What are the dimensions of the new bathroom?
   A) 4 × 10
   B) 8 × 10
   C) 10 × 10
   D) 4 × 8
   E) 8 × 8

321) In your job in the town planning and urban development office, you need to determine the area of a circular pond that the city is going to construct in the town park. The pond is to have a diameter of 36 feet. What figure below best approximates the area of the pond?
A) 1017
B) 804
C) 113
D) 57
E) 3069

322) You manufacture horse feed and equine nutritional products. One of your types of feed is sold by the half ton. This particular feed is shipped to a seller in the United Kingdom who needs to know the weight in grams. What figure should you state for the weight in grams?
A) 453,592
B) 45,359.2
C) 4,535.92
D) 45.3592
E) 2.20462

323) You need to report the amount of the average high temperature in your town over a three-month period in degrees Fahrenheit. However, the high temperatures are reported in Celsius. You have received the following data: January: 12°C; February: 13°C; March 17°C. What was the average high temperature for these three months in degrees Fahrenheit?
A) 57.2
B) 62.6
C) 82.8
D) 25.8
E) 32.4

324) You are overseeing the construction of a shopping center. A recent report states that 72.8% of the work for the shopping center is now completed, and it has taken 182 days to do so. If work continues at the same rate, approximately how many more days will be needed to finish the construction?
A) 17
B) 18
C) 58
D) 68
E) 250

325) You work in the fabricating division of a company that makes self-assembly furniture. You need to specify the diameter of the shaft of the screws for the product before manufacturing can begin. The diameter of the hole for each screw is specified as 0.250 inch with a tolerance of ±0.005 inch. The minimum diameter of the shaft of the screw must be 0.0025 inch larger than the maximum hole diameter so that the screw will grip the wood when the product is assembled. If the diameter of the shaft of the screw has a tolerance of ±0.0001 inch, what diameter in inches should you specify for the shaft of the screws?
A) 0.2555
B) 0.2576
C) 0.2550
D) 0.2754
E) 0.2755

Workkeys Practice Test 1 – Solutions and Explanations Level 3

1) The correct answer is C. The problem is asking for the total for all three years, so we add the three figures together: $25,135 + $32,787 + $47,004 = $104,926

2) The correct answer is D. For questions that ask you to calculate the change given to a customer, you need to take the amount of money the customer gives you and subtract the amount of the purchase: $50.00 – $41.28 = $8.72

3) The correct answer is E. Multiplication problems will often include the words 'each' or 'every.' The problem states that you earn a $175 referral fee on every customer, so you earned the referral fee 8 times this month. We need to multiply the amount of the referral fee by the number of customers to solve: $175 × 8 = $1400

4) The correct answer is C. Division problems will often include the word 'per.' The problem states that you work 30 hours per week. So, we divide the total weekly amount by the number of hours to solve: $535.50 ÷ 30 = $17.85

5) The correct answer is B. When you have to add a negative number to a positive number, you are really subtracting. So, add the business profits and subtract the business losses:
953 + 1502 – 286 – 107 = 2062

6) The correct answer is A. In this problem, we need to subtract the excess of the depth of Lake Bajo from the location below sea level of Lake Alto. The location below sea level of Lake Alto is a negative number, so we subtract as follows: –35 – 62 = –97. Remember to express your result as a negative number.

7) The correct answer is B. In order to express a fraction as a decimal, treat the line in the fraction as the division symbol: 3/5 = 3 ÷ 5 = 0.60. Be careful with the decimal placement in your final result.

8) The correct answer is C. To express a decimal number as a percent, move the decimal point two places to the right and add the percent sign: 0.55 = 55.0%

9) The correct answer is D. In order to express a fraction as a percentage, you need to divide and then express the result as a percentage. Step 1 – Treat the line in the fraction as the division symbol: 5/14 = 5 ÷ 14 = 0.357. Step 2 – To express the result from Step 1 as a percentage, we need to move the decimal point two places to the right and add the percent sign: 0.357 = 35.7%

10) The correct answer is E. For your exam, you should be able to recognize the equivalent fractions for commonly-used decimal numbers. If you are unsure, perform division on the answer choices to check:
3/4 = 3 ÷ 4 = 0.75

11) The correct answer is A. For your exam, you should be able to recognize the equivalent fractions for commonly-used percentages. If you are unsure, perform division on the answer choices to check:
1/3 = 1 ÷ 3 = 0.3333 = 33%

12) The correct answer is C. Any given percentage is out of 100%, so we divide by 100 to express a percentage as a decimal. So, move the decimal point two places to the left and remove the percent sign:
45% = 45 ÷ 100 = 0.45

13) The correct answer is B. Express both amounts as decimal numbers and multiply to solve: 14¼ pounds × 36 cents per pound = 14.25 × 0.36 = $5.13

14) The correct answer is C. There are 60 minutes in an hour, so multiply the minutes in the hour by the decimal number given in the problem to solve: 60 minutes × 0.35 hour = 60 × 0.35 = 21 minutes

Workkeys Practice Test 2 – Solutions and Explanations Level 4

15) The correct answer is A. Step 1 – Subtract the discount from the original price: $24 – $5 = $19. Step 2 – Take the result from Step 1 and multiply by the number of units sold: $19 × 12 = $228

16) The correct answer is D. Step 1 – Determine the total number of hours worked: 7 hours per day for 4 days = 7 × 4 = 28 hours. Step 2 – Calculate the profit your company makes per hour. The customer was billed $45 per hour for your work, and you were paid $25 per hour: $45 – $25 = $20 profit per hour. Step 3 – Multiply the total number of hours by the profit per hour to solve: 28 hours × $20 profit per hour 28 × 20 = $560

17) The correct answer is E. Step 1 – Calculate how many minutes there are in 40 hours: 40 hours × 60 minutes per hour = 2400 minutes. Step 2 – Divide the amount of prescriptions into the previous result to get the rate: 2400 ÷ 250 = 9.6 minutes per prescription

18) The correct answer is C. The orders that were delivered on time are part of the total order. So, take the amount of orders that were delivered on time and divide by the amount of total orders: 105 ÷ 120 = 0.875 = 87.5%

19) The correct answer is B. On Monday cell growth was 27, and for all of the days Tuesday through Friday, cell attrition was 13 per day. Step 1 – Cell attrition is a negative number, so perform multiplication to get the total for the four days (Tuesday through Friday): –13 × 4 = –52. Step 2 – On Monday cell growth was 27, so add this to the result from Step 1 to solve: –52 + 27 = –25

20) The correct answer is B. To find the average, you need to find the total, and then divide the total by the number of hours. Step 1 – Find the total: 23 + 25 + 26 + 24 + 22 = 120. Step 2 – Divide the result from Step 1 by the number of hours: 120 ÷ 5 = 24

21) The correct answer is D. Step 1 – Take the 66 units of cement powder for the current batch and divide by the 3 units stated in the original ratio: 66 ÷ 3 = 22. Step 2 – Multiply the result from Step 1 by the 2 units of sand stated in the original ratio to get your answer: 2 × 22 = 44

22) The correct answer is D. The problem states that we are working with a ratio, so the employees and the supervisors form separate groups. Step 1 – Add the two groups together: 50 + 1 = 51. Step 2 – Take the total amount of employees stated in the problem and divide this by the figure calculated in Step 1 to get the amount of supervisors: 255 ÷ 51 = 5

23) The correct answer is D. The problem uses the phrase '2 out of every 20 employees' so we know that there are 2 employees who form a subset within each group of 20. Step 1 – Take the total number of employees and divide this by 20: 480 ÷ 20 = 24. Step 2 – Take the result from Step 1 and multiply by the amount in the subset to solve: 24 × 2 = 48

24) The correct answer is E. Step 1 – Calculate the amount of time spent on the initial job to do 3 wheel covers: 8:10 to 8:22 = 12 minutes. Step 2 – Calculate how many minutes are needed to change 1 wheel cover: 12 minutes ÷ 3 = 4 minutes each. Step 3 – Divide the figure from Step 2 into 60 minutes to solve: 60 ÷ 4 = 15

25) The correct answer is C. Step 1 – Add the whole numbers. The whole numbers are the numbers in front of the fractions: 15 + 13 = 28. Step 2 – Add the fractions. If you have two fractions that have the same denominator, you add the numerators and keep the common denominator: 2/8 + 5/8 = 7/8. Step 3 – Combine the results from Step 1 and Step 2 to get your new mixed number to solve the problem: 28 + 7/8 = 28 7/8

26) The correct answer is A. Step 1 – Add the whole numbers: 2 + 4 = 6. Step 2 – Add the fractions. If you have two fractions that have the same denominator, you add the numerators and keep the common denominator: 1/8 + 3/8 = 4/8. Step 3 – Simplify the fraction from Step 2: 4/8 = (4 ÷ 4)/(8 ÷ 4) = 1/2. Step 4 – Combine the results from Step 1 and Step 3 to get your new mixed number to solve the problem: 6 + 1/2 = 6$\frac{1}{2}$

27) The correct answer is A. Step 1 – Subtract the whole numbers: 5 – 4 = 1. Step 2 – Subtract the fractions. If you have two fractions that have the same denominator, you subtract the numerators and keep the common denominator: 3/16 – 1/16 = 2/16. Step 3 – Simplify the fraction from Step 2: 2/16 = (2 ÷ 2)/(16 ÷ 2) = 1/8. Step 4 – Combine the results from Step 1 and Step 3 to get your new mixed number to solve the problem: 1 + 1/8 = 1$\frac{1}{8}$

28) The correct answer is B. Add the three figures together to solve: 0.25 + 0.50 + 0.10 = 0.85. Remember to be sure to put the decimal point in the correct place when you work out the solution to problems like this one.

29) The correct answer is C. Add the percentages together to solve: 25% + 50% = 75%

30) The correct answer is D. Step 1 – Multiply the whole numbers: 5 × 1 = 5. Step 2 – Multiply the whole number by the fraction: 5 × 1/4 = 5/4. Step 3 – Convert the fraction from Step 2 to a mixed number: 5/4 = 1$\frac{1}{4}$. Step 4 – Combine the results from Step 1 and Step 3 to get your new mixed number: 5 + 1$\frac{1}{4}$ = 6$\frac{1}{4}$. Step 5 – Convert the result from Step 4 to hours and minutes: 6$\frac{1}{4}$ hours = 6 hours and 15 minutes

31) The correct answer is D. Step 1 – Express the number of individual trips that have been taken or are in progress as a mixed number (2 × 2) + 1/2 = 4$\frac{1}{2}$ Step 2 – Multiply the mixed number from Step 1 by the decimal number for the miles for a single trip to solve: 100.75 × 4$\frac{1}{2}$ = 453.375 miles. which we round to 453 miles.

32) The correct answer is C. When determining how much to re-stock, it is most logical to start the inventory calculation with the beginning balance. So, you would take the beginning inventory and subtract the amount of sales to get the ending inventory. You would then take the desired amount of stock and subtract the ending inventory to get the amount of stock to replenish.

Workkeys Practice Test 3 – Solutions and Explanations Level 5

33) The correct answer is B. Step 1 – Convert the first fraction to the common denominator: $1/8 = (1 \times 4)/(8 \times 4) = 4/32$. Step 2 – Add one more increment to this to get your result: $4/32 + 1/32 = 5/32$

34) The correct answer is C. $198 + 15 = 213$ total customers, rather than 214 total customers.

35) The correct answer is E. From the formula sheet, we can see that 1 cubic yard = 27 cubic feet. To solve, multiply the amount of 60 cubic yards, stated in the question, by 27: $60 \times 27 = 1620$ cubic feet

36) The correct answer is B. From the formula sheet, we can see that 1 foot = 0.3048 meters. To solve, multiply the amount of 538 feet, stated in the question, by 0.3048: $538 \times 0.3048 = 163.98$, which we round up to 164.

37) The correct answer is D. Step 1 – Add the feet together: $123 + 138 = 261$ feet. Step 2 – Add the inches together: $6 + 8 = 14$ inches. Step 3 – Convert the inches to feet and inches if the result from Step 2 is 12 inches or more: 14 inches = 1 foot 2 inches. Step 4 – Combine the results from Step 1 and Step 3 to solve: 261 feet + 1 foot 2 inches = 262 feet 2 inches

38) The correct answer is A. Step 1 – Work out the cost for the first supplier: 50 units × $0.50 = $25. Step 2 – Compare to other deals to solve: The other deals are $27.50 and $30, so $25 is the best deal.

39) The correct answer is D. Step 1 – Determine the duration of your stay in weeks and nights: 9 nights = 1 week + 2 nights. Step 2 – Add the cost for 1 week to the cost for 2 days to solve: $280 + (2 × $45) = $280 + $90 = $370

40) The correct answer is E. From the formula sheet, we can see that the area of a circle ≈ 3.14 × (*radius*)^2. So, put in 12 feet for the radius to solve: $3.14 \times (12 \times 12) = 3.14 \times 144 = 452.16$

41) The correct answer is C. From the formula sheet, we know that the circumference of a circle ≈ 3.14 × diameter. The problem states that the diameter of the tractor tire is 46.5 inches, so use that in the formula to solve: $3.14 \times 46.5 = 146.01$ inches

42) The correct answer is E. The area of a rectangle = length × width. Your quilt is 6 feet long and 5 feet wide, so multiply to solve: $6 \times 5 = 30$

43) The correct answer is B. The perimeter of a rectangle = 2(length + width). Your field is 12 yards long and 9 yards wide, so use the formula to solve: $2(12 + 9) = 2 \times 21 = 42$

44) The correct answer is D. Step 1 – Determine the dollar value of the discount: $15 – $12 = $3. Step 2 – Divide the result from Step 1 by the original price to get the percentage: $3 ÷ $15 = 0.20 = 20%

45) The correct answer is E. Step 1 – Determine the dollar value of the markup on the mug: $9 retail price – $3 cost = $6 markup. Step 2 – Calculate the percentage of the markup by dividing the dollar value of the markup by the cost: $6 ÷ $3 = 2.00 = 200%. Step 3 – Use the percentage markup from the previous step to determine the dollar value of the markup on the bowl: $4 × 200% = $4 × 2 = $8. Step 4 – Add the dollar value of the markup for the bowl to the cost of the bowl to get the retail price: $8 + $4 = $12

Workkeys Practice Test 4 – Solutions and Explanations Level 6

46) The correct answer is E. To calculate a reverse percentage you need to divide, rather than multiply. So, take the $20 discount and divide by the 25% percentage: $20 ÷ 25% = $20 ÷ 0.25 = $80

47) The correct answer is A. Step 1 – Convert the weight of the full box from pounds and ounces to just ounces. Using the formula from the formula sheet, 1 pound = 16 ounces, so 8 pounds and 5 ounces = (8 × 16) + 5 = 128 + 5 = 133 ounces. Step 2 – The problem states that the box weighs 7 ounces when it is empty. So, subtract the weight of the empty box from the weight of the full box to get the weight of the product inside the box: 133 ounces – 7 ounces = 126 ounces. Step 3 – The problem tells us that each supplement weighs 0.75 ounces. Take the total weight from the previous step and divide by the weight per unit to determine how many units the box contains: 126 ounces ÷ 0.75 ounces = 168 units

48) The correct answer is C. Step 1 – Add the times for the first two processes and express in terms of hours and minutes: Production time of 3 hours and 25 minutes + Bottling and labeling time of 1 hour and 40 minutes = 3 hours + 1 hour + 25 minutes + 40 minutes = 4 hours and 65 minutes = 5 hours and 5 minutes. Step 2 – Add the time for the packaging process of 26 hours to the result from Step 1: 5 hours and 5 minutes + 26 hours = 31 hours and 5 minutes. Step 3 – Determine the time that the batch will be ready for shipment. 31 hours and 5 minutes have passed. In other words, a period of 24 hours and an additional 7 hours and 5 minutes have passed. The process started on Monday at 10:30 am, so by Tuesday at 10:30 am, 24 hours will have passed. An additional 7 hours and 5 minutes takes us to Tuesday at 5:35 pm.

49) The correct answer is B. From the formula sheet, we can see that the area of a rectangle is length × width. To get an erroneous result of 100 square feet, you would have had to multiply the width of 10 inches again by the width. So, you used width when you should have used length in the formula.

50) The correct answer is C. Step 1 – Determine the cost from the first supplier: 240 × 0.25 = $60. The tax on this will be $60 × 6.5% = $60 × 0.065 = $3.90. Then add the tax to the cost to get the total: $60 + $3.90 = $63.90. Step 2 – Determine the total cost from the second supplier: $58 cost + ($58 × 0.065 tax) = $58 + 3.77 = $61.77. So, you will get the better deal from the second supplier at $61.77.

51) The correct answer is B. Step 1 – The area of a circle ≈ 3.14 × radius^2. Here, we are given the area, so we have to divide by 3.14, instead of multiplying by 3.14, as stated in the formula: 78.5 ÷ 3.14 = 25. Step 2 – The result from the previous step is the radius squared. A squared number is the result of a number that has been multiplied by itself. 5 × 5 = 25, so the length of the radius of the pond is 5 feet. Step 3 – Remember that diameter is double the radius, so if the radius is 5, the diameter is 10 feet.

52) The correct answer is A. For questions on rearranging formulas like this one and the previous one, it is very likely that you are going to have to divide the largest number in the question by a smaller number in order to solve the problem. From the formula sheet, we know that the area of a rectangle = length × width. Here, we are given the area (the larger number of 360), so we need to divide that by the length (the smaller number of 30 feet) in order to get the width: 360 ÷ 30 = 12 feet

53) The correct answer is E. Step 1 – First we need to calculate the area in terms of square feet. The area of a circle ≈ 3.14 × radius^2. The diameter of the circle is 18 feet. Remember that radius is half of diameter, so the radius of the circle is 9 feet. So, the area is 3.14 × 9 × 9 = 254.34 square feet.
Step 2 – We have to convert the result from Step 1 to square inches. From the formula sheet, we can see that 1 square foot = 144 square inches, so multiply to solve: 254.34 × 144 = 36,624.96 square inches, which we round to 36,625.

54) The correct answer is D. Step 1 – Find the area in terms of square feet. Rectangular area = length × width. The cell is 14 feet long and 9 feet wide: 14 × 9 = 126 square feet. Step 2 – Convert the area in square feet to square yards. 1 square yard = 9 square feet. The formula converts square yards to square

feet, but we are converting square feet to square yards, so we need to divide by the conversion factor. So, divide by 9 to convert to yards: 126 ÷ 9 = 14 square yards

55) The correct answer is D. The volume of a rectangular solid = length × width × height. The tank is 5 feet wide, 8 feet long, and 3 feet high, so multiply to solve: 5 × 8 × 3 = 120

56) The correct answer is E. A cube is a three-dimensional object in which all sides have the same length. The volume of a cube = side length^3. So, put the length of the side in the formula to solve:
18 × 18 × 18 = 5832

57) The correct answer is D. Step 1 – Determine how many days are needed to make the small frames. You can make 20 small frames in 4 days: 20 frames ÷ 4 days = 5 small frames per day. The customer wants 40 small frames, so divide by the rate to determine how many days you are going to need for the small frames: 40 frames ÷ 5 per day = 8 days. Step 2 – Determine how many days you are going to need to make the large frames. You can make 21 larges frames in 3 days: 21 ÷ 3 = 7 large frames per day. You need to make 64 large frames for the order: 64 ÷ 7 = 9.1 days. Step 3 – Add the results from the two previous steps to solve: 8 days + 9.1 days = 17.1 days, which we round down to 17 days.

58) The correct answer is C. Step 1 – Calculate the percentage of work completed per day. 12.5% of the work has been completed in 4 days: 12.5 % ÷ 4 days = 3.125% per day. Step 2 – Determine how many days in total are needed to complete the entire job by dividing 100% by the result from the previous step: 100% ÷ 3.125% = 32 days. Step 3 – Determine the number of days remaining: 32 days in total – 4 days completed = 28 days remaining

59) The correct answer is B. There are 8 ounces in one cup, so if we had one cup of fluid, we would multiply by 8 to determine the volume in ounces. However, we are given the volume in cups, so we need to rearrange the formula, which means we need to divide 1 by 8 to determine the new formula. 1 ÷ 8 = 0.125. In other words, one ounce equals 0.125 cup, so our formula is: cups = fluid ounces × 0.125

60) The correct answer is A. Please notice that this problem is in the section entitled "Identifying the Correct Equations." So, you won't always have to rearrange a formula for questions of this type. Sometimes you only have to identify the equation. In this problem, the weights are taken in kilograms. We can see from our formula sheet that 1 kilogram is equal to 2.2 pounds, so we need to multiply kilograms by 2.2 to convert to pounds: pounds = kilograms × 2.2

Workkeys Practice Test 5 – Solutions and Explanations Level 7

61) The correct answer is B. Step 1 – Convert the mixed numbers to decimals and then multiply: $50\frac{1}{4}$ feet × $60\frac{1}{4}$ feet = 50.25 × 60.25 = 3027.5625 square feet. Step 2 – The price is given in square yards, so convert the square feet from the previous step to square yards. 1 square yard = 9 square feet, so 1/9 square yard = 1 square foot: 3027.5625 square feet ÷ 9 = 336.3958 square yards. Step 3 – Calculate the cost: 336.3958 × $5.25 = $1765.92, which we round to $1,766.

62) The correct answer is B. Step 1 – Calculate the amount of remaining stock in inches: (2 × 75 inches) + (4 × 25.25 inches) = 150 + 101 = 251 inches. Step 2 – Convert the existing stock from inches to yards: 1 foot = 12 inches and 1 yard = 3 feet, so there are 36 inches in 1 yard. So, divide the amount of inches by 36 to convert to yards: 251 ÷ 36 = 6.97 yards. Step 3 – Calculate the amount required to restock. 60 yards are required in total, and you have 6.97 yards on hand, so subtract to find out how many more yards you need to get the stock back up to 60 yards: 60 – 6.97 = 53.03 yards needed. Step 4 – The yarn comes in 5-yard balls, so calculate how many balls you need to buy to cover the 53.03 yards that are required: 53.03 ÷ 5 = 10.6 balls. It is not possible to buy a fractional part of a ball, so you have to buy 11 balls.

63) The correct answer is D. Step 1 – The clearance currently measures 0.34 mm with a 0.16 spacer in place, so when the spacer is taken out, the clearance would be 0.16 mm more, so we need to add these two amounts together to get our starting point: 0.34 mm + 0.16 mm = 0.50 mm. Step 2 – The clearance should be between 0.22 mm and 0.28 mm so subtract each of these from our previous figure to get the figures for the actual clearance: 0.50 mm – 0.22 mm = 0.28 mm and 0.50 mm – 0.28 mm = 0.22mm. Step 3 – The spacers come in 0.02 mm increments, so the 0.22 mm spacer would be suitable.

64) The correct answer is C. For these types of questions, you will usually have to take time to perform the calculations mentioned in each of the answer choices, but you may be able to eliminate some of the answer choices beforehand if you try the following steps first. Step 1 – Calculate the correct volume of the sphere. The volume of a sphere ≈ 4/3 × 3.14 × radius^3. The sphere is 6 feet across on the inside, so it has a radius of 3: 4/3 × 3.14 × 3^3 = 113.04 cubic feet. Step 2 – Compare the correct figure to the erroneous figure to determine whether the erroneous calculation was too large or too small. You calculated 904.32 cubic feet, so you erred on the large side. Step 3 – Identify where the error occurred. If you correctly used 4/3 and 3.14 from the formula, the only other possible error is in the measure of the radius. If you used 6 for the radius, you get the erroneous figure: 4/3 × 3.14 × 6^3 = 904.32 cubic feet

65) The correct answer is E. Step 1 – Convert 0.75 grams to milligrams. 1 milligram = 0.001 grams, so 0.75 grams ÷ 0.001 = 750 milligrams. Step 2 – The normal ratio is in the amount of 50 milligrams, so divide the result from the previous step by 50: 750 ÷ 50 = 15. So, you are using 15 times more active ingredient than normal. Step 3 – Determine the amount of liquid. Since you are using 15 times more of the active ingredient, you also need to use 15 times more of the liquid: 1.5 milliliters × 15 = 22.5 milliliters

66) The correct answer is C. 1 inch = 2.54 centimeters. Your current formula is (cost in dollars) = 0.12 × (length in inches), so you would have to multiply the measurement by the conversion factor to get the length in centimeters. When you have to multiply the measurement by the conversion factor, you then have to divide the price by the conversion factor. So, the international formula is: (cost in dollars) = 0.12 × (length in centimeters) ÷ 2.54 = 0.12 ÷ 2.54 × (length in centimeters) = 0.04724 × (length in centimeters)

67) The correct answer is A. Step 1 – Determine the cost for the first supplier: 725 pamphlets × 0.20 per pamphlet = $145. The tax on this is: $145 × 0.07 = $10.15, so the total cost is: $145 + $10.15 = $155.15. Step 2 – The total cost for the online order would be: $125 + 15 = $140, so this is the best price.

68) The correct answer is A. Step 1 – Calculate in cubic inches the volume of the sphere when it is full. The tank is 72 inches across on the inside, so the radius is 36 inches. The volume of a sphere ≈ 4/3 × 3.14 × radius^3: 4/3 × 3.14 × 36^3 = 195,333.12 cubic inches. Step 2 – Calculate in cubic inches how much

milk remains in the sphere. The tank is now 80% full of milk: 195,333.12 cubic inches × 0.80 = 156,266.50 cubic inches. Step 3 – Convert the cubic inches to gallons. 1 gallon = 231 cubic inches. The formula is gallons to cubic inches, but you are converting from cubic inches to gallons, so you need to divide: 156,266.50 cubic inches ÷ 231 = 676.48 gallons

69) The correct answer is E. The volume of a cylinder ≈ 3.14 × height × radius^2. Your tank has a 5 meter radius and is 21 meters in height: 3.14 × 21 × 5^2 = 3.14 × 21 × 25 = 1648.50 cubic meters

70) The correct answer is C. Step 1 – Calculate the volume of the large cone. The large cones are 6 inches high and have a 1.5 inch radius. The volume of a cone ≈ (3.14 × height × radius^2)/3 = (3.14 × 6 × 1.5 × 1.5)/3 = 14.13. Step 2 – Calculate the volume of the medium cone. The medium cones are 5 inches high and have a 1 inch radius: (3.14 × height × radius^2)/3 = (3.14 × 5 × 1 × 1)/3 = 5.23.
Step 3 – Calculate the difference between the volume of the two cones: 14.13 – 5.23 = 8.90

71) The correct answer is A. Step 1 – Calculate the diameter of the hole, within the tolerance. The diameter of each hole is specified as 0.800 inch with a tolerance of ±0.015 inch. With the tolerance, the diameter of the hole at its maximum could be 0.800 + 0.015 = 0.815, and at its minimum could be 0.800 – 0.015 = 0.785. Step 2 – Calculate the maximum diameter of the shaft of the rivet. The maximum diameter of the shaft of the rivet must be 0.003 inch smaller than the minimum hole diameter, so subtract this from the minimum figure from the previous step: 0.785 – 0.003 = 0.782. Step 3 – Calculate the diameter of the shaft of the rivet with a tolerance of ±0.0015 inch. The previous step shows a diameter of 0.782. Since this is the maximum diameter, a tolerance of +0.0015 is already included. So we deduct 0.0015 to get the diameter without the tolerance, which is 0.7805.

72) The correct answer is D. Step 1 – Calculate the dimensions of the floor in inches: 8 feet × 12 inches per foot = 96 inches long; 4 feet × 12 inches in a foot = 48 inches wide. Step 2 – Determine how many wooden pieces will fit along the length of the floor. If we lay the 12-inch side of the wooden piece against the length of the room, we can lay 8 of these side by side to cover the 96-inch length: 96 ÷ 12 = 8. Step 3 – Determine how many wooden pieces can fit along the width. 48-inch-wide floor ÷ 6-inch-wide pieces = 48 ÷ 6 = 8 pieces. Step 4 – Multiply the results from steps 2 and 3 to get the total number of pieces needed for the job: 8 × 8 = 64

73) The correct answer is D. To find the mean, add up all of the items in the set and then divide by the number of items in the set. Here we have 7 numbers in the set, so we get our answer as follows:
(89 + 65 + 75 + 68 + 82 + 74 + 86) ÷ 7 = 539 ÷ 7 = 77

74) The correct answer is A. The mode is the number that occurs the most frequently in the set. Our data set is: 1, 1, 3, 2, 4, 3, 1, 2, 1. The number 1 occurs 4 times in the set, which is more frequently than any other number in the set, so the mode is 1.

75) The correct answer is E. The mode is the number that occurs most frequently. However, if no number occurs more than once, the set has no mode.

76) The correct answer is B. The median is the number that is in the middle of the set when the numbers are in ascending order. The problem provides the number set: 8.19, 7.59, 8.25, 7.35, 9.10. First of all, put the numbers in ascending order: 7.35, 7.59, 8.19, 8.25, 9.10. Then find the one that is in the middle:
7.35, 7.59, **8.19**, 8.25, 9.10

77) The correct answer is C. To calculate the range, the low number in the set is deducted from the high number in the set. The problem set is: 98.5, 85.5, 80, 97, 93, 92.5, 93, 87, 88, 82. The high number is 98.5 and the low number is 80, so the range is 18.5: 98.5 – 80 = 18.5

78) The correct answer is B. We don't know the age of the 10th car, so put this in as x to solve:
$(2 + 3 + 4 + 5 + 6 + 7 + 9 + 10 + 12 + x) \div 10 = 6$
$[(2 + 3 + 4 + 5 + 6 + 7 + 9 + 10 + 12 + x) \div 10] \times 10 = 6 \times 10$
$2 + 3 + 4 + 5 + 6 + 7 + 9 + 10 + 12 + x = 60$
$58 + x = 60$
$x = 2$

79) The correct answer is C. If all of the values in a data set are positive integers greater than zero and all of the values increase, the mean and median will also increase, but the range will not change. Conversely, if all of the values in such a data set decrease, the mean and median will also decrease, but the range will not change. If each number in the set is increased by 2, the mean will increase by 2 since the overall increase in the total of the values (2 × 9 = 18) will be divided equally among all nine items in the set (18 ÷ 9 = 2) when the mean is calculated. Since each of the numbers increases by 2, the median number will also increase by 2.

80) The correct answer is A. Find the total points for the first group: 50 × 82 = 4100. Then find the total points for the second group. 50 × 89 = 4450. Add these two amounts together for the total points: 4100 + 4450 = 8550. Then divide the total points by the total number of members in the group: 8550 ÷ 100 = 85.5

Workkeys Practice Test 6 – Solutions and Explanations

81) The correct answer is E. Subtract the negative numbers as shown: –92 – 120 = –212. Remember to express your result as a negative number.

82) The correct answer is D. Remember that multiplication problems will often include the word 'every.' The problem states that you earn a $350 commission on every set of kitchen cupboards, so you earned the referral fee 11 times this week. We need to multiply the amount of the commission by the number of sets of cupboards to solve: $350 × 11 = $3850

83) The correct answer is B. The problem is asking for the total for all four months, so we add the four amounts together: $2516 + $3482 + $4871 + $5267 = $16,136

84) The correct answer is C. Divide the total amount by the number of members to solve:
$2,496 ÷ 52 = $48.

85) The correct answer is A. Take the amount of money the customer gives you and subtract the amount of the purchase: $150.00 – $127.82 = $22.18

86) The correct answer is E. Add the investment profits and subtract the business losses:
–$1205 + $532 + $875 – $1359 + $1436 – $982 = –$703

87) The correct answer is B. Treat the line in the fraction as the division symbol: $1/8$ = 1 ÷ 8 = 0.125

88) The correct answer is B. Divide and then express the result as a percentage. Step 1 – Treat the line in the fraction as the division symbol: 6/25 = 6 ÷ 25 = 0.24. Step 2 – To express the result from Step 1 as a percentage, move the decimal point two places to the right and add the percent sign: 0.24 = 24%

89) The correct answer is C. If you are unsure, perform division on the answer choices to check:
$4/5$ = 4 ÷ 5 = 0.8 = 80%

90) The correct answer is C. To express a decimal number as a percent, move the decimal point two places to the right and add the percent sign: 0.32 = 32.0%

91) The correct answer is B. Divide by 100 to express a percentage as a decimal. So, move the decimal point two places to the left and remove the percent sign: 25% = 25 ÷ 100 = 0.25

92) The correct answer is B. Multiply the total number of items by the decimal number given in the problem to solve: 50 items × 0.24 completed = 50 × 0.24 = 12 items

93) The correct answer is C. Perform division on the answer choices to check your answer:
1/5 = 1 ÷ 5 = 0.20

94) The correct answer is C. Multiply to solve: 15½ ounces × 20 cents per ounce = 15.50 × 0.20 = $3.10

Workkeys Practice Test 7 – Solutions and Explanations

95) The correct answer is C. Step 1 – Determine the amount of time worked in minutes: 35 hours × 60 minutes per hour = 2100 minutes. Step 2 – Divide by the amount of order forms to find the rate: 2100 minutes ÷ 210 order forms = 10 minutes each

96) The correct answer is D. Step 1 – Take the total number of families and divide this by 10, which is the number of families in the original ratio: 4500 ÷ 10 = 450. Step 2 – Take the result from Step 1 and multiply by the amount in the subset to solve: 450 × 7 = 3,150

97) The correct answer is E. Add to solve: –$1,503 + $2,476 – $3,087 + $986 = –$1,128

98) The correct answer is B. Step 1 – Add the gift wrap to the original price: $12 – $1.50 = $13.50. Step 2 – Take the result from Step 1 and multiply by the number of gifts sold: $13.50 × 51 = $688.50

99) The correct answer is C. Step 1 – Determine the total number of hours worked: 7 hours per day for 6 days = 7 × 6 = 42 hours. Step 2 – Calculate the profit your company makes per hour. The customer was billed $30 per hour for your work, and you were paid $18 per hour: $30 – $18 = $12 profit per hour. Step 3 – Multiply the total hours by the profit per hour to solve: 42 hours × $12 profit per hour = $504

100) The correct answer is D. Take the amount of satisfactory responses and divide by the amount of total customers: 132 ÷ 150 = 0.88 = 88.0%

101) The correct answer is A. To find the average, calculate the total, and then divide by the number of days. Step 1 – Find the total: 106 + 110 + 108 + 112 + 104 = 540. Step 2 – Divide the result from Step 1 by the number of days: 540 ÷ 5 = 108

102) The correct answer is D. Step 1 – Add the whole numbers: 5 + 3 = 8. Step 2 – Add the fractions: 5/8 + 3/8 = 8/8. Step 3 – Simplify the fraction from Step 2: 8/8 = 1. Step 4 – Combine the results from Step 1 and Step 3 to solve the problem: 8 + 1 = 9

103) The correct answer is A. Step 1 – Subtract the whole numbers: 10 – 9 = 1. Step 2 – Subtract the fractions: 7/12 – 5/12 = 2/12. Step 3 – Simplify the fraction from Step 2: 2/12 = 1/6. Step 4 – Combine the results from Step 1 and Step 3 to get your new mixed number to solve the problem: 1 + 1/6 = $1^{1/6}$. The amount after re-measuring was greater than the initial measurement, so $1^{1/6}$ yards more fabric is needed.

104) The correct answer is C. Step 1 – Add the whole numbers: 25 + 32 = 57. Step 2 – Add the fractions: 7/16 + 2/16 = 9/16. Step 3 – Combine the results from Step 1 and Step 2 to get your new mixed number to solve the problem: 57 + 9/16 = $57^{9/16}$

105) The correct answer is B. Step 1 – Take the 84 ounces for the mixture and divide by the 2 ounces of herbicide stated in the original ratio: 84 ÷ 2 = 42. Step 2 – Multiply the result from Step 1 by the 5 ounces of water stated in the original ratio to get your answer: 5 × 42 = 210

106) The correct answer is E. Step 1 – Take the total amount of mid-level managers stated in the problem and divide this by the 3 stated in the original ratio: 87 ÷ 3 = 29. Step 2 – Take the amount from Step 1 and multiply by the 2 upper-level managers from the original ratio to solve the problem: 29 × 2 = 58

107) The correct answer is E. Step 1 – Calculate the amount of time spent on the initial job: 9:15 to 9:35 = 20 minutes. Step 2 – Calculate the rate for 1 card: 20 minutes ÷ 2 cards made = 10 minutes per card. Step 3 – Determine how many minutes there are in 8 hours: 8 hours × 60 minutes = 480 minutes available. Step 4 – Divide the total minutes by the rate per card to solve: 480 total minutes ÷ 10 minutes per card = 48 cards

108) The correct answer is B. Add the three figures together to solve: 75.25 + 10.75 + 3.20 = 89.2

109) The correct answer is A. Add the percentages together to solve: 45% + 35% = 80%

110) The correct answer is D. Step 1 – Convert the mixed number to a decimal: $2^1/_2$ = 2.5 hours. Step 2 – Multiply this result by the number of units: 2.5 hours per unit × 5 units = 12.5 hours. Step 3 – Convert the decimal to minutes: 0.5 hour = 30 minutes. Step 4 – Express your answer in hours and minutes: 12 hours and 30 minutes

111) The correct answer is C. When determining how much has been sold, you are most likely start the calculation with the amount in stock at the beginning of the month. You would begin the calculation with the 105 pens at the start of the month, then add the 400 pens purchased, and then subtract the 350 pens left to find out how many pens you have sold.

112) The correct answer is D. Step 1 – Calculate the total amount of miles for the white lines for six years. There is a double white line, so we have to multiply by 2: 500 × 2 = 1,000 miles. Step 2 – Add in the amount for the yellow line = 1,000 + 200 = 1,200 miles total for six years. Step 3 – Double the result from the previous step to get the amount for 12 years: 1,200 × 2 = 2,400

Workkeys Practice Test 8 – Solutions and Explanations

113) The correct answer is A. Step 1 – Convert the first fraction to the common denominator: 5/8 = (5 × 2)/(8 × 2) = 10/16. Step 2 – Subtract one increment from this to get your result: 10/16 – 1/16 = 9/16

114) The correct answer is D. Step 1 – Determine the excess amount over the amount in the deal. 15 pairs needed – 12 pairs in the deal = 3 individual pairs remaining. Step 2 – Take the result from the previous step and multiply by the individual price: 3 × $1.50 = $4.50. Step 3 – Add the result from the previous step to the price for the 12 pairs in the deal to solve: $10 + 4.50 = $14.50

115) The correct answer is C. 1018 + 18 = 1036 total units produced, rather than 1026 total units produced.

116) The correct answer is B. Step 1 – Work out the cost for your usual supplier: 120 units × $172 = $20,640. Step 2 – Calculate the price for the third supplier: $19,000 + ($19,000 × .07) = $19,000 + $1,330 = $20,330. Step 3 – Compare to other deals to solve. The other deals are $20,640 and $20,500, so $20,330 is the best deal.

117) The correct answer is E. Step 1 – Add the cups: 2 cups + 3 cups = 5 cups. Step 2 – Convert the result from Step 1 to quarts and cups. There are 4 cups in one quart: 5 cups = 1 quart and 1 cup. Step 3 – Add the result from the previous step to the number of full quarts stated in the question: 3 quarts + 4 quarts + 1 quart and 1 cup = 8 quarts and 1 cup. Step 4 – Convert to gallons if possible. There are 4 quarts in one gallon: 8 quarts and 1 cup = 2 gallons and 1 cup

118) The correct answer is B. From the formula sheet, we can see that the area of a triangle is ½ (base × height). So, substitute the values to solve: ½ (base × height) = ½ (12 × 14) = ½ × 168 = 84 square inches

119) The correct answer is C. From the formula sheet, we know that the sum of the angles in a triangle is 180 degrees. So, subtract the measurements of the other two angles to solve: 180° – 47° – 44° = 89°

120) The correct answer is C. From the formula sheet, we can see that the area of a rectangle = length × width. Your wall is 16 feet by 11 feet, so multiply to solve: 16 × 11 = 176

121) The correct answer is B. From the formula sheet, we can see that 1 mile = 1.61 kilometers. So, multiply to solve: 38 miles × 1.61 = 61.18 kilometers, which we round to 61.

122) The correct answer is A. Step 1 – Determine the dollar value of the markup on the first bag: $12 retail price – $4 cost = $8 markup. Step 2 – Calculate the percentage of the markup on the first bag by dividing the dollar value of the markup by the cost: $8 ÷ $4 = 2.00 = 200%. Step 3 – Use the percentage markup from the previous step to determine the dollar value of the markup on the second style of bag: $3 × 200% = $3 × 2 = $6. Step 4 – Add the dollar value of the markup for the second style of bag to the cost of the bag to get the retail price: $3 + $6 = $9

123) The correct answer is D. From the formula sheet, we can see that a circle has 360 degrees. So, subtract to solve: 360 – 82 – 79 – 46 – 85 = 68

124) The correct answer is A. amps = watts ÷ volts. We have 780 watts and 120 volts, so use the formula to solve: 780 watts ÷ 120 volts = 6.5 amps

125) The correct answer is D. Step 1 – Determine the dollar value of the discount: $22.50 – $20 = $2.5. Step 2 – Divide the result from Step 1 by the original price to get the percentage: $2.50 ÷ $22.50 = 0.1111 = 11.11%, which we round to 11%.

Workkeys Practice Test 9 – Solutions and Explanations

126) The correct answer is B. Step 1 – Calculate the travel time remaining for the stops. There are 9 more stops, with travel time between stops of 6 minutes plus 2 minutes unloading: 9 × (6 + 2) = 9 × 8 = 72 minutes. Step 2 – Add the result from Step 1 to the 17 minutes travel time back to the school to get the total travel time remaining: 72 minutes + 17 minutes = 89 minutes. Step 3 – Add the result from Step 2 to the time now to determine the time that you will return back to the school: 3:38 pm + 89 minutes = 3:38 pm + 1 hour and 29 minutes = 4:38 pm + 29 minutes = 5:07 pm. Step 4 – Determine how much time you have to spare. You are supposed to return by 5:20 pm, and it will be 5:07 when you arrive, so you will arrive 13 minutes early.

127) The correct answer is C. Step 1 – Determine the cost from the first supplier: 350 × 0.85 = $297.50. The tax on this will be $297.50 × 8.5% = $25.29. Then add the tax to the cost to get the total: $297.50 + $25.29 = $322.79. Step 2 – Determine the total cost from the second supplier: $295 cost + ($295 × 0.085 tax) = $295 + 25.08 = $320.08. So, you will get the better deal from the second supplier at $320.08.

128) The correct answer is B. Step 1 – Find the volume in terms of cubic inches. Remember that radius is half of diameter. Here we have a diameter of 12, so the radius is 6. Cylinder volume ≈ 3.14 × radius^2 × height ≈ 3.14 × 6^2 × 18 ≈ 3.14 × 36 × 18 ≈ 2034.72. Step 2 – Convert the volume in cubic inches to gallons. 1 gallon = 231 cubic inches, so divide by 231 to convert to gallons: 2034.72 ÷ 231 = 8.8 gallons

129) The correct answer is D. To calculate a reverse percentage you need to divide, rather than multiply. So, take the $123 discount and divide by the 40% percentage: $123 ÷ 40% = $123 ÷ 0.40 = $307.50

130) The correct answer is A. Step 1 – Find the total weight of the product by subtracting the weight of the empty crate. The crate weighs 90 pounds and 12 ounces when it contains the product and 15 pounds when it is empty, so the product itself weighs: 90 pounds and 12 ounces – 15 pounds = 75 pounds and 12 ounces. Step 2 – Use the formula from the formula sheet to convert the total weight of the product from pounds and ounces to just ounces. 1 pound = 16 ounces, so 75 pounds and 12 ounces = (75 × 16) + 12 = 1200 + 12 = 1212 ounces. Step 3 – The problem tells us that each can of tomato sauce weighs 12 ounces. Take the total weight from the previous step and divide by the weight per unit to determine how many units the crate contains: 1212 ounces ÷ 12 ounces per unit = 101 units

131) The correct answer is A. Circumference ≈ 3.14 × diameter. In our problem, the radius is 12. Since the diameter is always double the radius, the diameter is 24. So, the circumference should be approximately 3.14 × 24 ≈ 75 square inches. Our result is much greater than this, so try to eliminate the answer choices one by one. The area of the circle ≈ 3.14 × radius^2 ≈ 3.14 × 12^2 ≈ 3.14 × 144 ≈ 452.16. So answer A is the correct choice.

132) The correct answer is A. From the formula sheet, we know that the volume of a rectangular solid = length × width × height. Here, we are given the volume (the larger number of 1080), so we need to divide that by the length and then the width in order to find the height: (1080 ÷ 12) ÷ 9 = 90 ÷ 9 = 10 feet

133) The correct answer is B. 1 foot = 0.3048 meters, so to convert to meters we need to multiply feet by 0.3048. 1 meter = 1,000 millimeters, so to convert from meters to millimeters, we need to multiply again by 1,000. So, the correct formula is as follows: millimeters = feet × 0.3048 × 1,000

134) The correct answer is A. In this problem, the measurements are taken in square yards. We can see from our formula sheet that 1 square yard = 9 square feet. The formula converts yards to feet, so we need to multiply square yards by 9 to convert to square feet. We can also see from the formula sheet that 1 acre = 43,560 square feet. However, this formula converts acres to square feet (rather than square feet to acres) so we need to divide the result from the previous step by 43,560 to calculate the acres. So, the correct formula is as follows: acres = (square yards × 9) ÷ 43,560

135) The correct answer is E. Step 1 – First we need to calculate the volume in terms of cubic feet. The volume of a cube = (length of side)^3. The length of the side is 9 feet, so the volume is 9 × 9 × 9 = 729 cubic feet. Step 2 – We have to convert the result from Step 1 to cubic inches. From the formula sheet, we can see that 1 cubic foot = 1,728 cubic inches, so multiply to solve: 729 × 1,728 = 1,259,712 cubic inches

136) The correct answer is A. 1 board foot = 1 inch by 12 inches by 12 inches, so substitute 14 for 1 to get 14 board feet. Alternatively, multiply the formula for board feet as follows: 1 board foot = 1 inch × 12 inches × 12 inches = 144 cubic inches. Then multiply by the amounts in the facts of our problems and divide by 144 to solve: (14 × 12 × 12) ÷ 144 = 14

137) The correct answer is B. Step 1 – Find the correct formula and conversion factor. The formula states that 1 kilowatt-hour = 1,000 watt-hours. The formula converts kilowatt-hours to watt-hours, but we want to convert watt-hours to kilowatt hours. So we need to divide by the conversion factor.
Step 2 – Divide to solve: 32,000 watt-hours ÷ 1,000 = 32 kilowatt-hours

138) The correct answer is E. Step 1 – Calculate the average high temperature in Fahrenheit. To do so, find the total for all five days and divide the result by 5: (72 + 68 + 65 + 82 + 81) ÷ 5 = 368 ÷ 5 = 73.6°F average. Step 2 – Convert the average in Fahrenheit to Celsius using the formula from the formula sheet. To convert Fahrenheit to Celsius, we use this formula: °C = 0.56(°F − 32) = 0.56(73.6° − 32) = 0.56(41.6) = 0.56 × 41.6 = 23.296, which we round to 23°C.

139) The correct answer is D. Step 1 – Determine the rate for the manicures: 5 hours ÷ 4 manicures = 1.25 hours per manicure = 1 hour and 15 minutes per manicure. Step 2 – Calculate the time needed for all 20 manicures: 1.25 hours per manicure × 20 manicures = 25 hours. Step 3 – Determine the rate for the pedicures: 2.5 hours ÷ 5 pedicures = 0.5 hours per pedicure. Step 4 – Calculate the time needed to do all 25 pedicures: 0.5 hours × 25 pedicures = 12.5 hours = 12 hours and 30 minutes.
Step 5 – Find the total for all of the manicures and pedicures: 25 hours + 12.5 hours = 37.5 hours = 37 hours and 30 minutes

140) The correct answer is C. Step 1 – Calculate the daily rate in terms of a daily percentage: 57.75% ÷ 7 days = 8.25% per day. Step 2 – Divide this amount into 100% to find the approximate number of days in total: 100% ÷ 8.25% per day = 12.12 days, which we round down to 12 days.

Workkeys Practice Test 10 – Solutions and Explanations

141) The correct answer is C. Step 1 – Determine the cost for the first supplier: 135 units × $15.30 per unit = $2,065.50. The tax on this is: $2,065.50 × 0.06 = $123.93, so the total cost is: $2,065.50 + $123.93 = $2189.43. Step 2 – The total cost for the other supplier is: $2,100 + 75 = $2,175. So, you will get the best price from the second company.

142) The correct answer is A. Step 1 – Calculate in cubic feet the volume of the container when it is full. The container is 25 feet long, 12 feet wide and 18 feet high. To find the volume of a rectangular solid, we use the formula: length × width × height = 25 × 12 × 18 = 5,400 cubic feet. Step 2 – Calculate in cubic feet how much product is in the container. The container is now 75% full: 5,400 cubic feet × 0.75 = 4,050 cubic feet. Step 3 – Convert the cubic feet to yards. 1 cubic yard = 27 cubic feet. The formula is cubic yards to cubic feet, but you are converting from cubic feet to cubic yards, so you need to divide: 4,050 cubic feet ÷ 27 = 150 cubic yards

143) The correct answer is C. Step 1 – Calculate the amount of remaining stock in quarts and ounces: [2 × (16 cups and 7 ounces)] + [3 × (20 cups and 4 ounces)] = 32 cups and 14 ounces + 60 cups and 12 ounces = 92 cups and 26 ounces. Step 2 – Convert the existing stock from cups to quarts: 1 quart = 4 cups, so divide the amount of cups by 4 to convert to quarts: (92 cups ÷ 4) + 26 ounces = 23 quarts and 26 ounces. There are 32 ounces in a quart, so we cannot convert the remaining 26 ounces to quarts. Step 3 – Calculate the amount required to restock. 50 quarts are required in total, and you have approximately 23 quarts on hand, so subtract to find out how many more quarts you need to get the stock back up to 50 quarts: 50 − 23 = 27 quarts needed. Step 4 – The chemical comes in 5-quart containers, so calculate how many containers you need to buy to cover the 27 quarts that are required: 27 ÷ 5 = 5.4 quarts. It is not possible to buy a fractional part of a container, so you have to buy 6 containers.

144) The correct answer is C. Step 1 – The clearance currently measures 0.46 mm with a 0.12 spacer setting in place, so when the spacer is taken out, the clearance would be 0.12 mm more, so we need to add these two amounts together to get our starting point: 0.46 mm + 0.12 mm = 0.58 mm. Step 2 – The clearance should be between 0.31 mm and 0.34 mm so subtract each of these from our previous figure to get the figures for the actual clearance: 0.58 mm − 0.31 mm = 0.27 mm and 0.58 mm − 0.34 mm = 0.24 mm. So, the actual clearance should be between 0.27 mm and 0.24 mm. Step 3 – The spacers come in 0.03 mm increments, so a spacer of 0.24 mm would be suitable.

145) The correct answer is D. Step 1 – Calculate the volume of each vat: length × width × height = 10 × 10 × 12 = 1,200 cubic feet. Step 2 – Determine how full each vat is in terms of cubic feet. Vat 1: 1,200 × $^3/_4$ = 1,200 × 0.75 = 900 cubic feet. Vat 2: 1,200 × $^4/_5$ = 1,200 × 0.80 = 960 cubic feet. Step 3 – Add the volume of the two vats together to determine the total volume: 900 + 960 = 1,860 cubic feet. Step 4 – Convert the cubic feet to cubic inches. 1 cubic foot = 1,728 cubic inches, so we multiply to convert: 1,860 cubic feet × 1,728 = 3,214,080 cubic inches. Step 5 – Multiply by the price to solve: 3,214,080 cubic inches × $0.12 = $385,689.60, which we round to $385,690.

146) The correct answer is E. Step 1 – Calculate the radius of the cone. The diameter is 6 and radius is half of diameter, so the radius is 3. Step 2 – Calculate the correct volume of the cone. The formula for the volume of a cone ≈ (3.14 × radius^2 × height) ÷ 3 = (3.14 × 3^2 × 8) ÷ 3 = 226.08 ÷ 3 = 75.36 cubic feet. Step 3 – Compare the correct figure to the erroneous figure to determine whether the erroneous calculation was too large or too small. You calculated 226 cubic feet, so you erred on the large side. Step 4 – Identify where the error occurred. We can see from the calculation in step 2 that final part of the calculation of the volume is (3.14 × 3^2 × 8) ÷ 3 = 226.08 ÷ 3, so you have forgotten to divide by 3.

147) The correct answer is A. 1 liter ≈ 0.264 gallons. Your current formula is (cost in cents) = 0.18 × (volume in gallons), but you will need to express it in liters. You are converting gallons to liters, so you would need to need to divide the gallons by 0.264 to get the volume in liters. Remember that if you divide the measurement by the conversion factor, you need to multiply the price by the conversion factor. So,

the international formula is: (cost in cents) = 0.18 × (volume in liters) × 0.264 = (0.18 × 0.264) × (volume in liters) = 0.0475 × (volume in liters)

148) The correct answer is B. Board feet is a measurement of volume, so keep that in mind as you work the formula. Step 1 – Find the volume of the lumber in terms of cubic feet. Your shipment is 26 feet by 14 feet by 10 feet: 26 × 14 × 10 = 3,640 cubic feet. Step 2 – Convert the cubic feet to cubic inches. 1 cubic foot = 1,728 cubic inches. 3,640 cubic feet × 1,728 = 6,289,920 cubic inches. Step 3 – Convert the formula for board feet. 1 board foot = 1 inch by 12 inches by 12 inches = 1 × 12 × 12 = 144 cubic inches. So, we need to divide our calculation for cubic inches by 144 to calculate board feet. Step 4 – Convert the cubic inches to board feet. 6,289,920 cubic inches ÷ 144 = 43,680 board feet. Step 5 – Calculate the cost for the product. $3.65 per board foot × 43,680 board feet = $159,432

149) The correct answer is A. To find the mean, add up all of the items in the set and then divide by the amount of items in the set. Here we have 8 scores, so we get our answer as follows:
(9.8 + 8.7 + 9.5 + 7.9 + 8.6 + 6.3 + 9.9 + 5.4) ÷ 8 = 66.1 ÷ 8 = 8.2625

150) The correct answer is C. The mode is the number that occurs the most frequently in the set. The number 325 occurs 2 times in the set, and the other numbers occur only once in the set, so the mode is 325.

151) The correct answer is A. The mode is the number that occurs the most frequently in the set. When no number occurs more than once, then there is no mode.

152) The correct answer is C. The median is the number that is in the middle of the set when the numbers are in ascending order. The problem provides the number set: 104, 103, 98, 102, 96, 100, 105. First of all, put the numbers in ascending order: 96, 98, 100, 102, 103, 104, 105. Then find the one that is in the middle: 96, 98, 100, **102**, 103, 104, 105.

153) The correct answer is B. No lights are to be installed in the corners, so each of the two 10-feet walls will have 1 light installed in the middle of each wall: 10 ÷ 5 = 2, but we subtract 1 from this for the corner. So, we have 1 light on each of the 2 shorter walls, which accounts for 2 lights so far. Each of the 25-foot walls have 5 increments of 5 feet, and again no lights are in the corners: (25 ÷ 5) – 1 = 4. So, each of the 2 long walls will have 4 lights on each wall. So there will be 10 lights in total on the walls in the room (1 + 1 + 4 + 4 = 10). You may wish to draw a diagram on your scratch paper when solving problems like this one.

154) The correct answer is D. Step 1 – Calculate the volume of the large ice cube: (1.8 × 1.8 × 1.8) = 5.832. Step 2 – Calculate the volume of the small ice cube: (1.4 × 1.4 × 1.4) = 2.744. Step 3 – Calculate the difference between the volume of the two ice cubes: 5.832 – 2.744 = 3.088

155) The correct answer is D. Step 1 – Calculate the area of the large triangle: (12 × 18) ÷ 2 = 216 ÷ 2 = 108. Step 2 – Calculate the area of the small triangle: (8 × 14) ÷ 2 = 112 ÷ 2 = 56. Step 3 – Subtract to solve: 108 – 56 = 52

Workkeys Practice Test 11 – Solutions and Explanations

156) The correct answer is C. The problem states that you get a $59 subscription for every new customer, so we need to multiply the amount of the subscription fee by the number of new customers to solve: $59 × 14 = $826

157) The correct answer is B. Treat the line in the fraction as the division symbol: $3/8 = 3 \div 8 = 0.375$

158) The correct answer is D. Perform the operation as shown: 35 – (–92) = 127. Express your result as a positive number since the value has increased from year 1 to year 2.

159) The correct answer is C. The problem is asking for the total for all three years, so we add the three amounts together: $ 12,225 + $43,871 + $ 69,423= $125,519

160) The correct answer is A. Take the amount of money the customer gives you and subtract the amount of the change provided to calculate the amount of the purchase: $75.00 – $8.35 = $66.65

161) The correct answer is C. Add to solve: –205 + 39 – 107 + 18 + 126 = –129

162) The correct answer is C. Step 1 – Determine the total number of hours worked: 7.5 hours per day for 2 days = 7.5 × 2 = 15 hours. Step 2 – Calculate the profit your company makes per hour. The customer was billed $75 per hour for your work, and you were paid $40 per hour: $75 – $40 = $35 profit per hour. Step 3 – Multiply the total number of hours by the profit per hour to solve: 15 hours × $35 profit per hour = $525

163) The correct answer is D. Step 1 – Add the whole numbers: 4 + 3 = 7. Step 2 – Add the fractions: 3/8 + 7/8 = 10/8. Step 3 – Simplify the fraction from Step 2: $10/8 = 8/8 + 2/8 = 1 + 2/8 = 1^{2}/_{8} = 1^{1}/_{4}$. Step 4 – Combine the results from Step 1 and Step 3 to solve the problem: $7 + 1^{1}/_{4} = 8^{1}/_{4}$

164) The correct answer is C. In this problem, the fraction on the second number is larger than the fraction on the first number, so we need to convert the first fraction before we start our calculation. Step 1 – Convert $12^{7}/_{16}$ for subtraction: $12^{7}/_{16} = 11^{7}/_{16} + 1 = 11^{7}/_{16} + {}^{16}/_{16} = 11^{23}/_{16}$. Step 2 – There were $8^{9}/_{16}$ yards left, so subtract the whole numbers: 11 – 8 = 3. Step 3 – Subtract the fractions: 23/16 – 9/16 = 14/16. Step 4 – Simplify the fraction from Step 3: 14/16 = (14 ÷ 2)/(16 ÷ 2) = 7/8. Step 4 – Combine the results from Step 2 and Step 4 to get your new mixed number to solve the problem: $3 + 7/8 = 3^{7}/_{8}$

165) The correct answer is B. The problem tells us the relative amount of units sold, but the question is asking for the relative amount of units left. So, subtract the decimal from 1 to find the relative amount left: 1 – 0.75 = 0.25. Then multiply the total number of items at the start by this decimal number: 80 items × 0.25 = 80 × 0.25 = 20 items left

166) The correct answer is B. In our problem, if $t\%$ subscribe to digital TV packages, then $100\% − t\%$ do not subscribe. In other words, since a percentage is any given number out of 100%, the percentage of students who do not subscribe is represented by this equation: $(100\% − t\%)$. This equation is then multiplied by the total number of students (n) in order to determine the number of students who do not subscribe to digital TV packages: $(100\% − t\%) \times n$

167) The correct answer is C. Step 1 – Set up the original proportion as a fraction. We have 3 parts of icing sugar for every 6 parts of sugar paste so our fraction is $3/6$. Step 2 – You can simplify the fraction from the previous step because both the numerator and denominator are divisible by 3: $3/6 \div 3/3 = 1/2$. Step 3 – We need to use 14 parts of sugar paste for the current batch, so multiply this amount by the simplified fraction. $1/2 \times 14 = 7$

168) The correct answer is E. This problem is asking for the ratio of non-faulty mp3 players to the quantity of faulty mp3 players. Therefore, you must put the quantity of non-faulty mp3 players before the colon in the ratio. In this problem, 1% of the players are faulty. 1% × 100 = 1 faulty player in every 100 players. 100 − 1 = 99 non-faulty players. So, the ratio is 99:1. The number before the colon and the number after the colon can be added together to get the total quantity.

169) The correct answer is B. The sales price of each cell phone is four times the cost. The cost is expressed as x, so the sales price is $4x$. The difference between the sales price of each cell phone and the cost of each cell phone is the markup. In this problem, the sales price is $4x$ and the cost is x.
Sales Price − Cost = Markup
$4x - x$ = Markup
$3x$ = Markup

170) The correct answer is D. The price of the internet connection is always 5 times the speed.
10 = 2 × 5
20 = 4 × 5
30 = 6 × 5
40 = 8 × 5
So, the price of the internet connection (represented by variable P) equals the speed (represented by variable s) times 5: $P = s \times 5$

171) The correct answer is C. To calculate the mean, add up all of the values: 1 + 2 + 3 + 4 + 5 + 5 + 8 + 8 + 9 = 45. There are 9 numbers in the set, so we need to divide by 9: 45 ÷ 9 = 5

172) The correct answer is C. To find the median, first you have to put the numbers in the data set in the correct order from lowest to highest: 3, 12, 18, **20**, 25, 28, 30. The median is the middle number in the set, which is 20 in this question.

173) The correct answer is C. In order to solve the problem, take the second equation and isolate J on one side of the equation. By doing this, you define variable J in terms of variable T.
$J + 2T = \$40$
$J + 2T - 2T = \$40 - 2T$
$J = \$40 - 2T$

Now substitute $\$40 - 2T$ for variable J in the first equation to solve for variable T.
$2J + T = 50$
$2(40 - 2T) + T = 50$
$80 - 4T + T = 50$
$80 - 3T = 50$
$80 - 3T + 3T = 50 + 3T$
$80 = 50 + 3T$
$80 - 50 = 50 - 50 + 3T$
$30 = 3T$
$30 \div 3 = 3T \div 3$
$10 = T$

So, now that we know that a T-shirt costs $10, we can substitute this value in one of the equations in order to find the value for the jeans, which is variable J.
$2J + T = 50$
$2J + 10 = 50$
$2J + 10 - 10 = 50 - 10$
$2J = 40$

$2J \div 2 = 40 \div 2$
$J = 20$

Now solve for the customer's purchase. If the customer purchased one pair of jeans and one T-shirt, then she paid: $10 + $20 = $30

174) The correct answer is B. Step 1 – Subtract one increment: 23/64 – 1/64 = 22/64. Step 2 – Simplify your result: 22/64 = (22 ÷ 2)/(64 ÷ 2) = 11/32

175) The correct answer is B. Step 1 – Work out the cost for your usual supplier: 325 pairs × $4 = $1,300. Step 2 – Calculate the price for the second supplier: $1,250 + ($1,250 × .06) = $1,250 + $75 = $1,325. Step 3 – Compare to the third deal to solve: The third deal is $1,290 so this is the best deal.

176) The correct answer is D. From the formula sheet, we can see that amps = watts ÷ volts. Here we have the amps, so we need to do the formula in reverse. So, we need to multiply to solve: 220 volts × 35 amps = 7,700 watts

177) The correct answer is C. We can see from the formula sheet that we have a formula to convert meters to centimeters and another formula to convert inches to centimeters, so we will need to use those two formulas to solve the problem. Step 1 – Determine the measurement in centimeters: 1 meter = 100 centimeters. Step 2 – Convert the centimeters to inches. The formulas states that 1 inch = 2.54 centimeters. However, we need to use the formula in reverse because we are converting centimeters to inches. So, divide to solve: 100 ÷ 2.54 = 39.37 inches

178) The correct answer is C. The sum of all three angles inside a triangle is always 180 degrees. So, we need to deduct the degrees given from 180° to find out the total degrees of the two other angles: 180° – 36° = 144°. Now divide this result by two in order to determine the degrees for each angle: 144° ÷ 2 = 72°

179) The correct answer is E. The area of a rectangle is equal to its length times its width. This football field is 30 yards wide and 100 yards long, so we can substitute the values into the appropriate formula.
rectangle area = width × length
rectangle area = 30 × 100
rectangle area = 3000

180) The correct answer is B. You are being asked about the distance around the outside, so you need to calculate the perimeter, Write out the formula: (length × 2) + (width × 2). Then substitute the values: (5 × 2) + (3 × 2) = 10 + 6 = 16

181) The correct answer is B. Substitute the value of the diameter into the formula to solve.
circumference ≈ diameter × 3.14
circumference ≈ 12 × 3.14

182) The correct answer is D. To calculate the volume of a box, you need the formula for a rectangular solid: volume = base × width × height. Now substitute the values from the problem into the formula.
volume = 20 × 15 × 25 = 7500

183) The correct answer is C. Step 1 – Determine the amount of seconds that have passed from 6:00 AM to 6:10 AM. 10 minutes × 60 seconds per minute = 600 seconds production time. Step 2 – Subtract the packaging time. 600 seconds – 5 seconds packaging per box = 595 seconds available for production. Step 3 – Determine the production time per unit: (9 seconds production time + 2 seconds set-up time) × 6 stages = 11 seconds × 6 = 66 seconds per unit. Step 4 – Divide the available production time by the time

per unit to determine how many items can be produced. 595 seconds ÷ 66 seconds = 9.015 units, which we round down to 9.

184) The correct answer is B. Step 1 – Find the total product weight, excluding the weight of the crate. 447 pounds – 60 pounds = 387 pounds. Step 2 – Convert the total product weight to ounces. 387 pounds × 16 ounces per pound = 6,192 ounces of total product weight. Step 3 – Convert the weight of each unit to ounces: 32 pounds and 4 ounces = (32 × 16) + 4 = 512 + 4 = 516 ounces each. Step 4 – Divide to solve: 6,192 ÷ 516 = 12 units

185) The correct answer is B. 1 kilometer = 0.62 miles, so we multiply the kilometers by 0.62 to get the miles. 1 mile = 5,280 feet, so we multiply the miles from the previous result by 5,280 to get the feet. So, the formula is: feet = (kilometers × 0.62) × 5,280

186) The correct answer is C. Step 1 – Determine the actual distance between the two cities in miles. 1 inch on the map = 20 miles, so 2.5 inches × 20 = 50 miles actual distance. Step 2 – Convert the result from Step 1 to kilometers. 1 mile = 1.61 kilometers, so 50 miles × 1.61 = 80.5 kilometers.

187) The correct answer is C. Step 1 – Determine the rate for the packaging: 1.5 hours ÷ 5 boxes = 90 minutes ÷ 5 boxes = 18 minutes per box. Step 2 – Add 4 extra minutes per box to the rate to account for the time to fill in the shipping form. 18 + 4 = 22 minutes per box needed in total. Step 3 – Calculate the time needed to package all 14 boxes and prepare them for shipment: 22 minutes × 14 = 308 minutes = 5 hours and 8 minutes

188) The correct answer is A. Step 1 – Calculate the amount of ounces needed to fill the small bottles: 25 bottles × 8 ounces each = 200 ounces. Step 2 – Calculate the amount of ounces needed to fill the large bottles: 20 bottles × 12 ounces each = 240 ounces. Step 3 – Add the ounces needed for the bottles and convert to quarts. There are 8 ounces in a cup, and there are 4 cups in a quart, so there are 32 ounces in a quart: 200 ounces + 240 ounces = 440 ounces ÷ 32 ounces in a quart = 13.75 quarts, which we round up to 14 quarts. Step 4 – Add the amount needed for the bottles to the amount required for stock: 14 quarts + 4 quarts = 18 quarts. Step 5 – Subtract the beginning stock from the total amount needed: 18 – 3 = 15 more quarts needed. The treatment is sold in 2 quart containers, so our result needs to be a multiple of 2, so we round up to 16 quarts, which equals 8 containers.

189) The correct answer is B. The volume of the container in cubic feet is calculated as follows: 9 × 5 × 6 = 270 cubic feet. We have to divide this by 27 to get the amount in cubic yards: 270 ÷ 3 27 = 10 cubic yards

Workkeys Practice Test 12 – Solutions and Explanations

190) The correct answer is B. Divide the total amount by the sales price per unit to solve: $7,375 ÷ $59 = 125 units sold

191) The correct answer is D. Add the growth and subtract the decreases: 52 – 14 + 37 – 28 + 61 = 108

192) The correct answer is C. Divide and then express the result as a percentage. Step 1 – Treat the line in the fraction as the division symbol: 6/25 = 6 ÷ 25 = 0.24. Step 2 – To express the result from Step 1 as a percentage, move the decimal point two places to the right and add the percent sign: 0.24 = 24.0%

193) The correct answer is A. 25% = 25/100 = ¼. If you are unsure, perform division on the answer choices to check.

194) The correct answer is C. Move the decimal point two places to the right and add the percent sign: 0.40 = 40.0%

195) The correct answer is D. First of all, you need to determine the difference in temperature during the entire time period: 62 – 38 = 24 degrees less. Then calculate how much time has passed. From 5:00 PM to 11:00 PM, 6 hours have passed. Next, divide the temperature difference by the amount of time that has passed to get the temperature change per hour: 24 degrees ÷ 6 hours = 4 degrees less per hour. To calculate the temperature at the stated time, you need to calculate the time difference. From 5:00 PM to 9:00 PM, 4 hours have passed. So, the temperature difference during the stated time is 4 hours × 4 degrees per hour = 16 degrees less. Finally, deduct this from the beginning temperature to get your final answer: 62°F – 16°F = 46°F

196) The correct answer is C. The number of hot dogs is D and the number of hamburgers is H. The equation to express the problem is: $(D \times \$2.50) + (H \times \$4) = \$22$. We know that the number of hamburgers is 3, so put that in the equation and solve it.
$(D \times \$2.50) + (H \times \$4) = \$22$
$(D \times \$2.50) + (3 \times \$4) = \$22$
$(D \times \$2.50) + 12 = \$22$
$(D \times \$2.50) + 12 - 12 = \$22 - 12$
$(D \times \$2.50) = \$10$
$\$2.50D = \$10$
$\$2.50D \div \$2.50 = \$10 \div \$2.50$
$D = 4$

197) The correct answer is C. For your first step, determine how many square feet there are in total: 2000 square feet per room × 8 rooms = 16,000 square feet in total. Then you need to divide by the coverage rate: 16,000 square feet to cover ÷ 900 square feet coverage per bucket = 17.77 buckets needed. It is not possible to purchase a partial bucket of paint, so 17.77 is rounded up to 18 buckets of paint.

198) The correct answer is E. Divide the distance traveled by the time in order to get the speed in miles per hour. Remember that in order to divide by a fraction, you need to invert the fraction, and then multiply.
3.6 miles ÷ ¾ =
3.6 × 4/3 =
(3.6 × 4) ÷ 3 =
14.4 ÷ 3 = 4.8 miles per hour

199) The correct answer is C. Step 1 – Determine the dollar amount of the reduction or discount: $60 original price – $45 sale price = $15 discount. Step 2 – Then divide the discount by the original price to get the percentage of the discount: $15 ÷ $60 = 0.25 = 25%

200) The correct answer is B. For your first step, add the subsets of the ratio together: 6 + 7 = 13. Then divide this into the total: 117 ÷ 13 = 9. Finally, multiply the result from the previous step by the subset of males from the original ratio: 6 × 9 = 54 males in the class

201) The correct answer is B. First add up all of the values: 1 + 1 + 3 + 2 + 4 + 3 + 1 + 2 + 1 = 18
There are nine values, so we divide to get the mean: 18 ÷ 9 = 2

202) The correct answer is D. Set up your equation to calculate the average, using x for the age of the 5th sibling:
$(2 + 5 + 7 + 12 + x) ÷ 5 = 8$
$(2 + 5 + 7 + 12 + x) ÷ 5 × 5 = 8 × 5$
$(2 + 5 + 7 + 12 + x) = 40$
$26 + x = 40$
$26 – 26 + x = 40 – 26$
$x = 14$

203) The correct answer is B. The problem provides the number set: 8.19, 7.59, 8.25, 7.35, 9.10.
First of all, put the numbers in ascending order: 7.35, 7.59, 8.19, 8.25, 9.10. Then find the one that is in the middle: 7.35, 7.59, **8.19**, 8.25, 9.10

204) The correct answer is C. For 2 sandwiches, the total price is $17.50, so each sandwich in this deal sells for $8.75: $17.50 total price ÷ 2 sandwiches = $8.75 each. For 4 sandwiches, the total price is $34.40, so each sandwich in this deal sells for $8.60: $34.40 total price ÷ 4 sandwiches = $8.60 each. For 8 sandwiches, the total price is $68, so each sandwich in this deal sells for $8.50: $68 total price ÷ 8 sandwiches = $8.50 each. So, the best price per sandwich is $8.50.

205) The correct answer is B. First, determine the total sales value of the cheese and pepperoni pizzas based on the prices stated in the problem: (15 cheese pizzas × $10 each) + (10 pepperoni pizzas × $12 each) = $150 + $120 = $270. The remaining amount is allocable to the vegetable pizzas: Total sales of $310 – $270 = $40 worth of vegetable pizzas. The problems states that 5 vegetable pizzas were sold. We calculate the price of the vegetable pizzas as follows: $40 worth of vegetable pizzas ÷ 5 vegetable pizzas sold = $8 per vegetable pizza

206) The correct answer is C. At the beginning of the year, 15% of the 1,500 creatures were fish, so there were 225 fish at the beginning of the year (1,500 × 0.15 = 225). In order to find the percentage of fish at the end of the year, we first need to add up the percentages for the other animals: 40% + 23% + 21% = 84%. Then subtract this amount from 100% to get the remaining percentage for the fish: 100% – 84% = 16%. Multiply the percentage by the total to get the number of fish at the end of the year: 1,500 × 0.16 = 240. Then subtract the beginning of the year from the end of the year to calculate the increase in the number of fish: 240 – 225 = 15

207) The correct answer is C. Shanika wants to earn $4,000 this month. She gets the $1,000 basic pay regardless of the number of cars she sells, so we need to subtract that from the total first: $4,000 – $1,000 = $3,000. She gets $390 for each car she sells, so we need to divide that into the remaining $3,000: $3,000 to earn ÷ $390 per car = 7.69 cars to sell. Since it is not possible to sell a part of a car, we need to round up to 8 cars.

208) The correct answer is D. First, we can perform division to determine that the plane travels 6.5 miles per minute: 780 miles ÷ 120 minutes = 6.5 miles per minute. Since the plane travels at a constant speed, we multiply this amount by 40 minutes to solve: 6.5 miles per minute × 40 minutes = 260 miles

209) The correct answer is D. Step 1 – Determine the amount of time in seconds: 2 minutes and 48 seconds = (2 minutes × 60 seconds per minute) + 48 seconds = 120 seconds + 48 seconds = 168 seconds. Step 2 – Divide by the amount of furlongs to find the rate: 168 seconds ÷ 12 furlongs = 14 seconds per furlong

210) The correct answer is C. Step 1 – Take the total number of viewers and divide this by the 100 viewers in the original ratio: 3200 ÷ 100 = 32. Step 2 – Take the result from Step 1 and multiply by the amount in the subset to solve: 32 × 30 = 960

211) The correct answer is E. Step 1 – Add the charge for postage and handling to the original price per item: $22 + $ 3 = $25. Step 2 – Take the result from Step 1 and multiply by the number of items sold: $25 × 32 = $800

212) The correct answer is B. Step 1 – Add the whole numbers: 107 + 96 = 203. Step 2 – Add the fractions: 3/8 + 1/8 = 4/8 = 1/2. Step 3 – Combine the results from Step 1 and Step 2 to get your new mixed number to solve the problem: 203 + 1/2 = 203 1/2

213) The correct answer is C. Add the four figures together to solve: 163.75 + 107.50 + 91.25 + 10.30 = 372.80

214) The correct answer is A. You would need to calculate the amount of lace needed to make all 6 dresses before you start the job, in order to see if you have enough lace on hand. The other data is only in the question to distract you.

215) The correct answer is B. Step 1 – The original order was for 5 quilts and this has been doubled, so we need enough fabric for 10 quilts: 5 × 2 = 10 quilts. Step 2 – Find the amount of material needed for each quilt: 2 yards red, 4 yards blue, 1.2 yards gold (6 ÷ 5 = 1.2), and 0.5 yards white = 2 + 4 + 1.2 + 0.5 = 7.7 yards each. Step 3 – Multiply the total number of quilts by the amount of yards per quilt to solve: 10 × 7.7 = 77

216) The correct answer is C. Each panel is 8 feet 6 inches long, and you need 11 panels to cover the entire side of the field. So, we need to multiply 8 feet 6 inches by 11. Step 1 – 8 feet × 11 = 88 feet. Step 2 – 6 inches × 11 = 66 inches. Step 3 – Now simplify the result. There are 12 inches in a foot, so we need to determine how many feet and inches there are in 66 inches. 66 inches ÷ 12 = 5 feet 6 inches. Step 4 – Add the two results together. 88 feet + 5 feet 6 inches = 93 feet 6 inches.

217) The correct answer is C. Since we are dealing with a square, all four sides of the floor are equal to each other. The tiles are also square, so they also have equal sides. Therefore, we can simply divide to get the answer: 64 ÷ 4 = 16

218) The correct answer is A. The volume of a cylinder is calculated as follows: volume ≈ 3.14 × (radius)^2 × height ≈ 3.14 × (5)^2 × 10 ≈ 785

219) The correct answer is A. First, we need to calculate the volume of cone A: (3.14 × 9^2 × 18) ÷ 3 = 1526.04. Then, we need to calculate the volume of Cone B: (3.14 × 3^2 × 6) ÷ 3 = 56.52. Then divide to get the ratio: 1526.04 ÷ 56.52 = 27. So, we can express the ratio as: $^{27}/_1$ = 27

220) The correct answer is E. The disallowed responses plus the valid responses equal the surveys received in each line of the report, so there is no mistake.

221) The correct answer is C. Step 1 – Determine the cost from the first supplier: 500 × 0.72 = $360.00. The tax on this will be $360.00 × 5.5% = $19.80. Then add the tax to the cost to get the total: $360.00 + $19.80 = $379.80. Step 2 – Determine the total cost from the second supplier: $350 cost + ($350 × 0.055 tax) = $350 + 19.25 = $369.25. So, you will get the better deal from the second supplier at $369.25.

222) The correct answer is A. 1 kilogram = 1,000 grams, so we need to multiply the kilograms by 1,000 to get the grams. 1 ounces = 28.53 grams, so we need to divide the grams by 28.53 to get the ounces because we are using the second formula in reverse.

223) The correct answer is C. Step 1 – Calculate the possible diameter of the piston. The diameter of the cylinder is 12 cm, and it needs a clearance between 0.03 to 0.06 cm, so subtract these amounts to calculate the possible values for the diameter of the piston: 12 cm – 0.03 cm = 11.97 and 12 cm – 0.06 cm = 11.94 cm. So, the diameter of the piston can be between 11.94 and 11.97 cm. Step 2 – The piston is currently 12.6 cm in diameter, and the reducing device is set to 0.18 cm. So, if we were to use the current setting, we would get a diameter of 12.6 – 0.18 = 12.42 cm. Step 3 – Deduct the possible values for the diameter of the piston from the value you have just calculated: 12.42 – 11.94 = 0.48 and 12.42 – 11.97 = 0.45. So, the setting on the device needs to be increased by a value between 0.45 cm and 0.48 cm. Step 4 – The settings are in increments of 0.03 cm, so divide the measurement of one increment into the values calculated in the previous step to find out how many increments are needed: 0.48 ÷ .03 = 16 and 0.45 ÷ 0.03 = 15. So, the setting on the device needs to be increased by 15 or 16 increments.

Workkeys Practice Test 13 – Solutions and Explanations

224) The correct answer is C. Move the decimal point two places to the left and remove the percent sign: 42% = 42 ÷ 100 = 0.42

225) The correct answer is C. Perform division on the answer choices to check your answer: 1/5 = 1 ÷ 5 = 0.20

226) The correct answer is D. Convert the cups to quarter cups: 10 cups = 40 quarter cups. Then combine the whole number with the fraction and multiply to solve: 40¼ × 50 cents per quarter cup = 40.25 × 0.50 = $20.50

227) The correct answer is A. Take the amount of money the customer gives you and subtract the amount of change provided to calculate the amount of the purchase: $160.00 − $12.64 = $147.36

228) The correct answer is C. The problem is asking for the total for all five months, so we add the amounts together to solve: $723 + $618 + $576 + $812 + $984 = $3,713

229) The correct answer is B. Treat the line in the fraction as the division symbol: 2/5 = 2 ÷ 5 = 0.40

230) The correct answer is C. Step 1 – Take the total number of employees and divide this by 5: 250 ÷ 5 = 50. Step 2 – The question asks how many questionnaires have not been completed and returned, so subtract to find the amount in the 'not returned' subset: 5 − 4 = 1. Step 3 – Multiply the result from step 2 by the result from step 1 to solve: 50 × 1 = 50

231) The correct answer is D. Step 1 – Determine the total for sales in December: $20 × 55 = $1,100. Step 2 – Determine the total sales for January: $12 × 20 = $240. Step 3 – Add these two amounts to solve: $1,100 + $240 = $1,340

232) The correct answer is A. The problem tells us that the morning flight had 52 passengers more than the evening flight, and there were 540 passengers in total on the two flights that day. Step 1 – First of all, we need to deduct the difference from the total: 540 − 52 = 488. In other words, there were 488 passengers on both flights combined, plus the 52 additional passengers on the morning flight.
Step 2 – Now divide this result by 2 to allocate an amount of passengers to each flight: 488 ÷ 2 = 244 passengers on the evening flight. (Had the question asked you for the amount of passengers on the morning flight, you would have had to add back the amount of additional passengers to find the total amount of passengers for the morning flight: 244 + 52 = 296 passengers on the morning flight)

233) The correct answer is C. Divide and then round up: 82 people in total ÷ 15 people served per container = 5.467 containers. We need to round up to 6 since we cannot purchase a fractional part of a container.

234) The correct answer is D. The question is asking us about a time duration of 6 minutes, so we need to calculate the amount of seconds in 6 minutes: 6 minutes × 60 seconds per minute = 360 seconds in total. Then divide the total time by the amount of time needed to make one journey: 360 seconds ÷ 45 seconds per journey = 8 journeys. Finally, multiply the number of journeys by the amount of inches per journey in order to get the total inches: 10.5 inches for 1 journey × 8 journeys = 84 inches in total

235) The correct answer is B. First of all, add up to find the total number of customers: 40 + 30 + 20 + 30 = 120 customers in total for all four regions. The salespeople received $540 in total, so we need to divide this by the amount of customers: $540 ÷ 120 customers = $4.50 per customer

236) The correct answer is B. The mean is the arithmetic average. First, find the total for all seven companies: –2% + 5% + 7.5% + 14% + 17% + 1.3% + –3% = 39.8%. Then divide by 7 since there are 7 companies in the set: 39.8% ÷ 7 = 5.68% ≈ 5.7%

237) The correct answer is D. The plumber is going to earn $4,000 for the month. He charges a set fee of $100 per job, and he will do 5 jobs, so we can calculate the total set fees first: $100 set fee per job × 5 jobs = $500 total set fees. Then deduct the set fees from the total for the month in order to determine the total for the hourly pay: $4,000 – $500 = $3,500. He earns $25 per hour, so divide the hourly rate into the total hourly pay in order to determine the number of hours he will work: $3,500 total hourly pay ÷ $25 per hour = 140 hours to work

238) The correct answer is E. Set up each part of the problem as an equation. The museum had twice as many visitors on Tuesday (T) as on Monday (M), so T = 2M. The number of visitors on Wednesday exceeded that of Tuesday by 20%, so W = 1.20 × T. Then express T in terms of M for Wednesday's visitors: W = 1.20 × T = 1.20 × 2M = 2.40M. Finally, add the amounts together for all three days: M + 2M + 2.40M = 5.4M

239) The correct answer is B. 45% of the freshman, 30% of the sophomores, 38% of the juniors, and 30% of the seniors will attend. Since each of the four grade levels has roughly the same number of students, we can simply divide by 4 to get the average. Calculating the average, we get the overall percentage for all four grades: (45 + 30 + 38 + 30) ÷ 4 = 35.75%. 35% is the closest answer to 35.75%, so it best approximates our result.

240) The correct answer is C. Step 1 – Determine the commission you earn per hour: $15 charged – $12 paid to employee = $3 per hour commission. Step 2 – Calculate the total hours that the 10 employees worked: 10 × 40 = 400 hours in total. Step 3 – Multiply the total number of hours by the commission per hour to solve: 400 hours × $3 commission per hour = $1,200 total commission

241) The correct answer is D. Divide to solve: 49 ÷ 50 = 0.98 = 98%

242) The correct answer is D. Calculate the total, and divide by the number of days. Step 1 – Find the total: $90 + $85 + $85 + $105 + $110 = $475. Step 2 – Divide the result from Step 1 by the number of days: $475 ÷ 5 = $95

243) The correct answer is D. Step 1 – Add the whole numbers: 8 + 7 = 15. Step 2 – Add the fractions: 3/4 + 1/2 = 3/4 + 2/4 = 5/4. Step 3 – Simplify the fraction from Step 2: 5/4 = 4/4 + 1/4 = 1¼ = 1 foot and 3 inches. Step 4 – Combine the results from Step 1 and Step 3 to solve the problem: 15 feet + 1 foot and 3 inches = 16 feet and 3 inches

244) The correct answer is C. In this problem, the fraction on the second number is larger than the fraction on the first number, so we need to convert the first fraction before we start our calculation.
Step 1 – Convert 28³/₁₀ for subtraction: 28³/₁₀ = 27³/₁₀ + 1 = 27³/₁₀ + ¹⁰/₁₀ = 27¹³/₁₀. Step 2 – Subtract the whole numbers. You have spent 7⁹/₁₀ hours on the job so far, so subtract the 7 hours: 27 – 7 = 20.
Step 3 – Subtract the fractions: 13/10 – 9/10 = 4/10. Step 4 – Simplify the fraction from Step 3: 4/10 = (4 ÷ 2)/(10 ÷ 2) = 2/5. Step 4 – Combine the results from Step 2 and Step 4 to get your new mixed number to solve the problem: 20 + 2/5 = 20²/₅

245) The correct answer is C. Step 1 – Take the 147 parts of blue slate chippings for this order and divide by the 3 parts stated in the original ratio: 147 ÷ 3 = 49. Step 2 – Multiply the result from Step 1 by the 2 parts of white gravel stated in the original ratio to get your answer: 49 × 2 = 98

246) The correct answer is C. Step 1 – Determine the total amount of inches of material needed for one unit. Don't forget that the second material needs to be doubled because there is a double layer of this

material: 18 + 19 + 19 = 56 inches. Step 2 – Calculate how many inches are needed in total: 56 inches per unit × 18 units = 1008 inches in total. Step 3 – Convert the inches to feet: 1008 inches ÷ 12 = 84 feet

247) The correct answer is D. Step 1 – Determine the excess amount over the amount for the deal: 100 bottles needed – (4 cases × 24 bottles each) = 100 – 96 = 4 individual bottles left. Step 2 – Take the result from the previous step and multiply by the individual price: 4 × $2.50 = $10. Step 3 – Determine the cost of the 4 cases: 4 × $50 = $200. Step 4 – Add the results from the previous two steps to get the total wholesale price for the deal: $200 + $10 = $210

248) The correct answer is E. Step 1 – Convert the grams to ounces: 1190.7 ÷ 28.35 = 42. Step 2 – Add the result from step 1 to the amount of ounces for the US order to solve: 39 + 42 = 81 ounces

249) The correct answer is E. Step 1 – Find the area of the ceiling. From the formula sheet, we can see that the area of a rectangle is (length × width). So, substitute the values to find the area: (35 × 25) = 875 square feet. Step 2 – Find the area of each ceiling tile. The measurements for our tiles are given in inches: 6 inches by 6 inches = 36 square inches. Step 3 – Calculate how many square inches there are in a square foot: 12 inches by 12 inches = 144 square inches. Step 4 – Determine how many tiles you need per square foot: 144 square inches ÷ 36 square inches per tile = 4 tiles per square foot. Step 5 – Multiply to solve: 875 square feet in total × 4 tiles per square foot = 3,500 tiles needed

250) The correct answer is B. From the formula sheet, we can see that 1 milligram = 0.001 gram. We are converting milligrams to grams, so we are doing the formula in the correct order, rather than in reverse. Therefore, multiply by 0.001 to solve: 1,275,000 milligrams × 0.001 = 1,275 grams

251) The correct answer is D. Step 1 – Find the radius in centimeters. The diameter is 10 inches, so the radius is 5 inches. 1 inch = 2.54 centimeters, so multiply to determine the length of the radius in centimeters: 5 × 2.54 = 12.7 centimeters. Step 2 – Cube the radius for the formula: 12.7 × 12.7 × 12.7 = 2048.38. Then multiply by 3.14 and 4/3 to find the volume of the sphere: 2048.38 × 3.14 × 4/3 = 8575.8968, which we round up to 8,576.

252) The correct answer is B. To calculate a reverse percentage you need to divide, rather than multiply. So, take the $12 retail price and divide by 625%, which is 100% for the cost plus 525% for the markup: $12 ÷ 625% = $12 ÷ 6.25 = $1.92

253) The correct answer is A. Convert Fahrenheit to Celsius: °C = 0.56(°F – 32). If we do the conversion correctly, we get 29.68°C: 0.56(85 – 32) = 0.56 × 53 = 29.68°C. If we divide by 0.56 instead of multiplying, we get the erroneous conversion of 94.64.

254) The correct answer is D. The perimeter of rectangle is 2(*length* + *width*). So, determine the total width for both sides: 2 × 75 = 150. Now deduct this amount from the perimeter: 350 – 150 = 200. Finally, divide this result by 2 to get the length: 200 ÷ 2 = 100

255) The correct answer is D. Step 1 – Calculate the cubic inches for each box: length × width × height = 3 × 3 × 2 = 18 cubic feet per box × 1,728 cubic inches per cubic foot = 31,104 cubic inches per box. Step 2 – Determine how much of the product is on hand. The first box is $1/6$ full, the second box is $1/2$ full, and the third box is $2/3$ full: $1/6 + 1/2 + 2/3 = 1/6 + 3/6 + 4/6 = 8/6$ = $1 2/6$ = $1 1/3$ boxes left. Step 3 – Determine how much is required to replenish the stock: 3 boxes needed – $1 1/3$ boxes on hand = $1 2/3$ boxes needed. Step 4 – Determine how many cubic inches are needed: $1 2/3$ boxes needed × 31,104 cubic inches per box = 51,840 cubic inches needed. Step 5 – Calculate the cost of the cubic inches: 51,840 cubic inches needed × 0.09 per cubic inch = $4,665.60, which we round to $4,666.

256) The correct answer is A. 1 inch = 2.54 centimeters. We would have to multiply the inches by 2.54 to get the correct measurement and divide the price by 2.54 to get the correct price. So, the international formula is: (cost in dollars) = 0.535 ÷ 2.54 × (length in centimeters) = 0.21063 × (length in centimeters)

Workkeys Practice Test 14 – Solutions and Explanations

257) The correct answer is C. The question is asking for the change from week 3 to week 4, so subtract week 3 from week 4 as shown: −5 − (−12) = −5 + 12 = 7

258) The correct answer is C. The problem states that you get a $12 commission for every order greater than $100, so we need to multiply the amount of the commission by the number of orders over $100 first of all: $12 × 32 = $384. Then add this to the basic pay to get the total for the month: $1250 + $384 = $1634

259) The correct answer is B. Divide the total amount of sales by the price per unit to solve:
$310 ÷ $12.40 = 25 units sold

260) The correct answer is A. Divide to check your answer: 10% = 10/100 = $1/10$

261) The correct answer is E. The ratio of bags of apples to bags of oranges is 2 to 3, so for every two bags of apples, there are three bags of oranges. First, take the total amount of bags of apples and divide by the 2 from the original ratio: 44 ÷ 2 = 22. Then multiply this by 3 to determine how many bags of oranges are in the store: 22 × 3 = 66

262) The correct answer is B. At the beginning of January, there are 300 students, but 5% of the students leave during the month, so we have 95% left at the end of the month: 300 × 95% = 285. Then 15 students join on the last day of the month, so we add that back in to get the total at the end of January: 285 + 15 = 300. If this pattern continues, there will always be 300 students in the academy at the end of any month.

263) The correct answer is D. Calculate the discount: $120 × 12.5% = $15 discount. Then subtract the discount from the original price to determine the sales price: $120 − $15 = $105

264) The correct answer is A. The ratio of defective chips to functioning chips is 1 to 20. So, the defective chips form one group and the functioning chips form another group. Therefore, the total data set can be divided into groups of 21. Accordingly, $1/21$ of the chips will be defective. The factory produced 11,235 chips last week, so we calculate as follows: 11,235 × $1/21$ = 535

265) The correct answer is B. The total amount available is $55,000, so we can substitute this for C in the equation provided in order to calculate R number of residents:
C = $750R + $2,550
$55,000 = $750R + $2,550
$55,000 − $2,550 = $750R + $2,550 − $2,550
$55,000 − $2,550 = $750R
$52,450 = $750R
$52,450 ÷ $750 = $750R ÷ $750
$52,450 ÷ $750 = R
69.9 = R
It is not possible to accommodate a fractional part of one person, so we need to round down to 69 residents.

266) The correct answer is B. Our data set is: 2.5, 9.4, 3.1, 1.7, 3.2, 8.2, 4.5, 6.4, 7.8. First, put the numbers in ascending order: 1.7, 2.5, 3.1, 3.2, 4.5, 6.4, 7.8, 8.2, 9.4. The median is the number in the middle of the set: 1.7, 2.5, 3.1, 3.2, **4.5**, 6.4, 7.8, 8.2, 9.4

267) The correct answer is D. To find the mean, add up all of the items in the set and then divide by the number of items in the set. Here we have 7 numbers in the set, so we get our answer as follows:
(89 + 65 + 75 + 68 + 82 + 74 + 86) ÷ 7 = 539 ÷ 7 = 77

268) The correct answer is E. We don't know the age of the 8th car, so put this in as x to solve:
$(2 + 3 + 4 + 5 + 9 + 10 + 12 + x) \div 8 = 6$
$[(2 + 3 + 4 + 5 + 9 + 10 + 12 + x) \div 8] \times 8 = 6 \times 8$
$2 + 3 + 4 + 5 + 9 + 10 + 12 + x = 48$
$45 + x = 48$
$x = 3$

269) The correct answer is C. The fine for speeding is $50 per violation, so the total amount collected for speeding violations was: 60 speeding violations × $50 per violation = $3000. There 90 other violations, and the fine for other violations is $20, so the total for other violations is: 90 × $20 = $1800. Next, we need to deduct these two amounts from the total collections of $6,000 in order to find out how much was collected for parking violations: $6000 – $3000 – $1800 = $1200 in total for parking violations. There were 30 parking violations. We divide to get the answer: $1200 income for parking violations ÷ 30 parking violations = $40 each

270) The correct answer is E. The original price of the sofa on Wednesday was x. On Thursday, the sofa was reduced by 10%, so the price on Thursday was 90% of x or $0.90x$. On Friday, the sofa was reduced by a further 15%, so the price on Friday was 85% of the price on Thursday, so we can multiply Thursday's price by 0.85 to get our answer: $(0.90)(0.85)x$

271) The correct answer is C. If the amount earned from selling jackets was one-third that of selling jeans, the ratio of jacket to jean sales was 1 to 3. So, we need to divide the total sales of $4,000 into $1,000 for jackets and $3,000 for jeans. We can then solve the problem as follows: $3,000 in jeans sales ÷ $20 per pair = 150 pairs sold

272) The correct answer is D. Move the decimal point two places to the left and remove the percent sign: 81% = 81 ÷ 100 = 0.81

273) The correct answer is C. 0.35 = 35/100 = (35 ÷ 5)/(100 ÷ 5) = 7/20. Perform division on the answer choices to check your answer: 7/20 = 7 ÷ 20 = 0.35

274) The correct answer is A. Step 1 – Add the whole numbers: 37 + 25 = 62. Step 2 – Add the fractions: 2/5 + 4/5 = 6/5 = 1 1/5. Step 3 – Combine the results from Step 1 and Step 2 to get your new mixed number to solve the problem: 62 + 1 1/5 = 63 1/5

275) The correct answer is C. Step 1 – Take the total amount of customers expected and divide by the 3 stated in the original ratio: 15 ÷ 3 = 5. Step 2 – Take the amount from Step 1 and multiply by 1 from the original ratio to solve the problem: 5 × 1 = 5

276) The correct answer is D. Step 1 – Calculate the amount of time spent on the initial job: 9:15 AM to 10:25 AM = 1 hour and 10 minutes = 70 minutes. Step 2 – Calculate the rate per square yard: 70 minutes ÷ 7 square yards = 10 minutes per square yard. Step 3 – Multiply the figure from Step 2 by the total amount of square yards to paint: 17.5 square yards × 10 minutes per square yard = 175 minutes = 2 hours and 55 minutes. Step 4 – Determine the time of completion: 9:15 AM + 2 hours and 55 minutes = 11:15 AM + 55 minutes = 12:10 PM

277) The correct answer is E. Add the three figures together to solve: 1235.35 + 567.55 + 347.25 = 2150.15 units

278) The correct answer is D. Step 1 – Add the whole numbers: 19 + 14 = 33. Step 2 – Add the fractions: 3/4 + 3/4 = 6/4. Step 3 – Simplify the fraction from Step 2: 6/4 = 1 2/4 = 1 1/2. Step 4 – Combine the results from Step 1 and Step 3 to solve the problem: 33 + 1 1/2 = 34 1/2

279) The correct answer is A. In this problem, the fraction on the second number is larger than the fraction on the first number, so we need to convert the first fraction before we start our calculation. Step 1 – Convert the first mixed number for subtraction: $102^{7}/_{18} = 101^{7}/_{18} + 1 = 101^{7}/_{18} + {}^{18}/_{18} = 101^{25}/_{18}$. Step 2 – Subtract the whole numbers: 101 – 24 = 77. Step 3 – Subtract the fractions: 25/18 – 11/18 = 14/18. Step 4 – Simplify the fraction from Step 3: 14/18 = (14 ÷ 2)/(18 ÷ 2) = 7/9. Step 5 – Combine the results from Step 2 and Step 4 to get your new mixed number to solve the problem: 77 + 7/9 = $77^{7}/_{9}$.

280) The correct answer is C. Step 1 – Convert the mixed number to minutes: $1^{3}/_{4}$ = 1 hour and 45 minutes = 105 minutes. Step 2 – Multiply the 15 minutes by the 14 patients: 15 × 14 = 210 minutes. Step 3 – Add the results from steps 1 and 2: 105 + 210 = 315 minutes. Step 4 – Calculate how many minutes there are in 8 hours × 60 = 480 minutes. Step 5 – Determine how much time you have left: 480 minutes available – 315 minutes on tasks = 165 minutes left. Step 6 – Convert this to hours and minutes: hours: 165 minutes = 2 hours and 45 minutes

281) The correct answer is D. Calculate the total, and divide by the number of employees. Step 1 – Find the total: 96 + 89 + 63 + 98 + 81 + 77 = 504. Step 2 – Divide the result from Step 1 by the number of employees: 504 ÷ 6 = 84

282) The correct answer is D. Circumference ≈ diameter × 3.14. The circumference of the first circle is calculated as follows: diameter × 3.14 = 10 × 3.14 = 31.4. The circumference of the second circle is as follows: diameter × 3.14 = 6 × 3.14 = 18.84. The difference in the circumferences is: 31.4 – 18.84 = 12.56

283) The correct answer is B. Circumference is diameter × 3.14, so the circumference of the large tire is 20 × 3.14 = 62.80, and the circumference of the smaller tire is 12 × 3.14 = 37.68. If the large tire travels 360 revolutions, it travels a distance of approximately 22,608, since 62.80 × 360 = 22,608. To determine the number of revolutions the small tire needs to make to go the same distance, we divide the distance by the circumference of the smaller tire: 22,608 ÷ 37.68 = 600. Finally, calculate the difference in the number of revolutions: 600 – 360 = 240

284) The correct answer is C. Perimeter = 2L + 2W = (2 × 18) + (2 × 10) = 36 + 20 = 56

285) The correct answer is C. From the formula sheet, we know that the circumference of a circle is approximately 3.14 times the diameter. The partition is going to divide the circular arena in half, so the partition will be placed on the diameter of the circle. So divide to calculate the measurement in feet of the diameter: 1,017.36 ÷ 3.14 = 324 feet. We need to express the result in yards, so divide by 3 to solve: 324 ÷ 3 = 108 yards

286) The correct answer is D. Step 1 – Determine the percentage of the discount on Product A: $4 discount ÷ $20 original price = 20% discount. Step 2 – Calculate the dollar value of the discount on Product B: $16 × 20% = $3.20. Step 3 – Subtract the dollar value of the discount on Product B from the normal price to get the discounted price of Product B: $16 - $3.20 = $12.80

287) The correct answer is E. Step 1 – First we need to calculate the volume in terms of cubic inches. 10 inches × 7 inches × 5 inches = 350 cubic inches. Step 2 – Convert the cubic inches to gallons. 1 gallon = 231 cubic inches, so divide by 231 to get the gallons: 350 ÷ 231 = 1.5151 gallons, which we round to 1.52 gallons.

288) The correct answer is D. Step 1 – The formula states that 1 kilowatt-hour = 1,000 watt-hours. So, multiply to solve: 1,200 × 1,000 = 1,200,000

289) The correct answer is C. Step 1 – Determine the cost for Supplier A: 210 units × $3.25 per unit = $682.50. The tax on this is: $682.50 × 0.05 = $34.125, which we round to $34.13. So the total cost for Supplier A is: $682.50 + $34.13 = $716.63 Step 2 – The total cost for Supplier B is: $695 + 25 = $720. So, you will get the best price of $716.63 from Supplier A.

290) The correct answer is D. Step 1 – Take the 14 cups for this batch and divide by the 2 cups stated in the original ratio: 14 ÷ 2 = 7. Step 2 – Multiply the result from Step 1 by the 3 ounces of herbal therapy product stated in the original ratio to get your answer: 3 × 7 = 21

291) The correct answer is C. Step 1 – Convert the mixed number to a decimal: $1\frac{1}{4}$ = 1.25 hours. Step 2 – Multiply the result from the previous step by the number of intervals: 1.25 × 7 = 8.75 hours. Step 3 – Convert the decimal to minutes: 0.75 hour = 45 minutes. Step 4 – Express your answer in hours and minutes: 8 hours and 45 minutes

Workkeys Practice Test 15 – Solutions and Explanations

292) The correct answer is D. Add the gains and subtract the setbacks as shown:
−14 + 52 − 36 − 7 = −5

293) The correct answer is C. Divide and then express the result as a percentage. Step 1 – Treat the line in the fraction as the division symbol: 9/16 = 9 ÷ 16 = 0.5625. Step 2 – To express the result from Step 1 as a percentage, move the decimal point two places to the right and add the percent sign: 0.5625 = 56.25%

294) The correct answer is C. Move the decimal point two places to the right and add the percent sign: 0.95 = 95.0%

295) The correct answer is E. Subtract the decimal from 1 to find the decimal amount left: 1 − 0.05 = 0.95. Then multiply the total number of employees at the start of the year by this decimal number: 120 × 0.95 = 114 employees left

296) The correct answer is D. 20 percent is equal to 0.20. We are doing a reverse percentage, so we need to divide to solve: $60 ÷ 0.20 = $300. We can check this result as follows: 300 × 0.20 = 60

297) The correct answer is A. First, subtract whole numbers: 6 − 2 = 4. Then subtract fractions: $3/4 - 1/2 = 3/4 - 2/4 = 1/4$. Put them together for the result: $4 1/4$

298) The correct answer is B. Set up the proportion as a fraction: 9 ounces of liquid for every 6 of ounces active chemical = $9/6$. Then simplify the fraction: $9/6 ÷ 3/3 = 3/2$. Now, multiply the fraction by the amount for the current job to solve: $3/2 × 10 = 30/2 = 30 ÷ 2 = 15$

299) The correct answer is B. First you need to find the total points. You do this by taking the erroneous average times 5: 5 × 96 = 480. Then you need to divide the total points earned by the correct number of surveys to get the correct average: 480 ÷ 6 = 80

300) The correct answer is E. You have 3 partial trays of unsold brownies at the end of the day, and each tray has $1/8$ of the brownies left in it, so in total you have $3/8$ of a tray left. You need to divide this by 4 employees. When you are asked to divide fractions, remember that you need to invert the second fraction. Here we have the whole number 4. 4 inverted is $1/4$. So, multiply the fractions to solve: $3/8 × 1/4 = {(3 × 1)}/{(8 × 4)} = 3/32$

301) The correct answer is E. Represent the mixed numbers as decimal numbers: Person 1: $14 3/4$ = 14.75; Person 2: $20 1/5$ = 20.20; Person 3: 36.35. Then add all three amounts together to find the total: 14.75 + 20.20 + 36.35 = 71.30

302) The correct answer is C. You purchased 50 reams of paper to use in your office this month and have used 5 of them, so you need to divide to solve 5 ÷ 50 = 0.10

303) The correct answer is D. First of all, you have to calculate the total amount of points earned by the entire group. Multiply the female average by the amount of female candidates. Total points for females: 87 × 55 = 4785. Then multiply the male average by the amount of males. Total points for male candidates: 80 × 45 = 3600. Then add these two amounts together to find out the total points scored by the entire group. Total points for entire group: 4785 + 3600 = 8385. When you have calculated the total amount of points for the entire group, you divide this by the total number of candidates to get the average: 8385 ÷ 100 = 83.85

304) The correct answer is E. We know that Mary has already gotten 80% of the money. However, the question is asking how much money she still needs: 100% − 80% = 20% = 0.20. Now do the multiplication: 650 × 0.20 = 130

305) The correct answer is B. They buy 4 of product A at $5 each, so they buy $20 worth of product A. They paid $60 in total, so subtract the total cost of product A from the overall total to calculate the total spent on Product B: $60 − $20 = $40. Product B costs $8 each, so divide to solve: $40 spent on Product B ÷ $8 each = 5 units

306) The correct answer is C. She bought 3 pairs of shoes, so determine the amount spent on shoes: 3 pairs of shoes × $25 each = $75. Then deduct this from the total amount of the purchase to calculate how much she spent on socks: $85 − $75 = $10. The socks cost $2 a pair, so divide to solve: $10 ÷ $2 each = 5 pairs

Alternatively, we can say that the number of pairs of socks is S and the number of pairs of shoes is H. The equation is: $(S \times \$2) + (H \times \$25) = \$85$. We know that the number of pairs of shoes is 3, so put that in the equation and solve it.
$(S \times \$2) + (H \times \$25) = \$85$
$(S \times \$2) + (3 \times \$25) = \$85$
$(S \times \$2) + \$75 = \$85$
$(S \times \$2) + 75 - 75 = \$85 - \$75$
$(S \times \$2) = \$10$
$\$2S = \$10$
$\$2S \div 2 = \$10 \div 2$
$S = 5$

307) The correct answer is C. Step 1 – Determine the price per yard: $10.50 per 1/2 yard × 2 = $21.00 per yard. Step 2 – Calculate the price for 20 yards: 20 × $21.00 = $420.00. Step 3 – The customer purchased 20 and a half yards, so the price of the remaining half yard is $10.50. Add this to the result from Step 2 to get your answer: $420.00 + $10.50 = $430.50

308) The correct answer is D. Step 1 – Add the whole numbers: 49 + 18 = 67. Step 2 – Add the fractions: 3/16 + 1/16 = 4/16 = 1/4. Step 3 – Combine the results from Step 1 and Step 2 to get your new mixed number to solve the problem: 67 + 1/4 = 67 1/4

309) The correct answer is B. Take the amount of defective chips and divide by the amount of total chips: 11 ÷ 132 = 0.083 = 8.3%, which we round to 8%.

310) The correct answer is E. Step 1 – Take the total amount of flour required for this batch and divide by the 9 stated in the original ratio: 126 ÷ 9 = 14. Step 2 – Take the amount from Step 1 and multiply by 2 from the original ratio to solve the problem: 14 × 2 = 28

311) The correct answer is B. Step 1 – Calculate the amount of time spent on the initial job: 12:10 to 2:25 = 2 hours and 15 minutes = 135 minutes. Step 2 – Calculate the rate per cap: 135 minutes ÷ 3 caps = 45 minutes per cap. Step 3 – Calculate how many minutes there are in 9 hours: 9 hours × 60 minutes = 540 minutes. Step 4 – Divide to solve: 540 minutes available ÷ 45 minutes per cap = 12 caps

312) The correct answer is D. Add the percentages together to solve: 58% + 27% = 85%

313) The correct answer is C. The circumference of a circle is calculated by using this formula: Circumference ≈ 3.14 × diameter. The diameter of a circle is always equal to the radius times 2. So, the diameter for this circle is 4 × 2 = 8. Therefore, the approximate circumference is: 3.14 × 8 = 25.12

314) The correct answer is D. Area of a circle ≈ 3.14 × radius². The radius of this circle is 6, and 6² = 36. Therefore, the area is approximately: 36 × 3.14 = 113.04

315) The correct answer is B. The area of circle A is 0.4² × 3.14 = 0.16 × 3.14 = 0.5024. The area of circle B is 0.2² × 3.14 = 0.04 × 3.14 = 0.1256. Then subtract: 0.5024 − 0.1256 = 0.3768

316) The correct answer is D. The volume of a box is calculated by taking the length times the width times the height: 5 × 6 × 10 = 300

317) The correct answer is B. Triangle area = (base × height) ÷ 2. Substitute the amounts for base and height: area = (5 × 2) ÷ 2 = 10 ÷ 2 = 5

318) The correct answer is B. Cone volume = (3.14 × radius² × height) ÷ 3. Substitute the values for base and height. volume = (3.14 × 3² × 4) ÷ 3 = (3.14 × 9 × 4) ÷ 3 = 3.14 × 36 ÷ 3 = 37.68

319) The correct answer is B. Remember that the perimeter is the measurement along the outside edges of the rectangle or other area. The formula for perimeter is as follows: P = 2W + 2L. If the room is 12 feet by 10 feet, we need 12 feet × 2 to finish the long sides of the room and 10 feet × 2 to finish the shorter sides of the room. (2 × 10) + (2 × 12) = 20 + 24 = 44. Each piece of wood is one foot long, so 44 pieces are needed to finish the room.

320) The correct answer is A. First, we have to calculate the total square footage available.
If there are 4 rooms which are 10 by 10 each: 4 × (10 × 10) = 400 square feet in total

Now calculate the square footage of the new rooms.
20 × 10 = 200
2 rooms × (10 × 8) = 160
200 + 160 = 360 total square feet for the new rooms

So, the remaining square footage for the bathroom is calculated by taking the total minus the square footage of the new rooms: 400 − 360 = 40 square feet left

Since each existing room is 10 feet long, we know that the new bathroom also needs to be 10 feet long in order to fit in. So, the new bathroom is 4 feet × 10 feet.

321) The correct answer is A. The area of a circle is 3.14 × radius². Radius is half of diameter, and in our problem the diameter is 36, so the radius is 18. So, put the values into the formula to solve: 3.14 × 18 × 18 = 1,017

322) The correct answer is A. 1 ton is 2,000 pounds, so a half ton is 1,000 pounds. 1 pound = 453.592 grams, so multiply to solve: 1,000 × 453.592 = 453,592

323) The correct answer is A. Step 1 – Calculate the average high temperature in Celsius: (12 + 13 + 17) ÷ 3 = 42 ÷ 3 = 14°C average. Step 2 – Convert the average in Celsius to Fahrenheit using the formula from the formula sheet. °F = 1.8(°C) + 32 = 1.8(14°) + 32 = 25.2 + 32 = 57.2° F.

324) The correct answer is D. Step 1 – Calculate the rate in terms of a daily percentage: 72.8% ÷ 182 days = 0.4% per day. Step 2 – Divide this amount into 100% to find the approximate number of days in total: 100% ÷ 0.4% per day = 250 days in total. Step 3 – Subtract to determine how many days remain: 250 − 182 = 68 days left

325) The correct answer is B. Step 1 – Calculate the diameter of the hole, within the tolerance. The diameter of each hole is specified as 0.250 inch with a tolerance of ±0.005 inch. With the tolerance, the diameter of the hole at its maximum could be 0.250 + 0.005 = 0.255, and at its minimum could be 0.250 – 0.005 = 0.245. Step 2 – Calculate the maximum diameter of the shaft of the rivet. The minimum diameter of the shaft of the screw must be 0.0025 inch larger than the maximum hole diameter, so add this to the maximum figure from the previous step: 0.255 + 0.0025 = 0.2575. Step 3 – The minimum diameter of the shaft of the screw already includes the tolerance of -0.0001 inch, so add back 0.0001 inch to solve: 0.2575 + 0.0001 = 0.2576

ANSWER KEY

1) C

2) D

3) E

4) C

5) B

6) A

7) B

8) C

9) D

10) E

11) A

12) C

13) B

14) C

15) A

16) D

17) E

18) C

19) B

20) B

21) D

22) D

23) D

24) E

25) C

26) A

27) A

28) B
29) C
30) D
31) D
32) C
33) B
34) C
35) E
36) B
37) D
38) A
39) D
40) E
41) C
42) E
43) B
44) D
45) E
46) E
47) A
48) C
49) B
50) C
51) B
52) A
53) E
54) D
55) D

56) E

57) D

58) C

59) B

60) A

61) B

62) B

63) D

64) C

65) E

66) C

67) A

68) A

69) E

70) C

71) A

72) D

73) D

74) A

75) E

76) B

77) C

78) B

79) C

80) A

81) E

82) D

83) B

84) C

85) A

86) E

87) B

88) B

89) C

90) C

91) B

92) B

93) C

94) C

95) C

96) D

97) E

98) B

99) C

100) D

101) A

102) D

103) A

104) C

105) B

106) E

107) E

108) B

109) A

110) D

111) C

112) D

113) A

114) D

115) C

116) B

117) E

118) B

119) C

120) C

121) B

122) A

123) D

124) A

125) D

126) B

127) C

128) B

129) D

130) A

131) A

132) A

133) B

134) A

135) E

136) A

137) B

138) E

139) D

140) C
141) C
142) A
143) C
144) C
145) D
146) E
147) A
148) B
149) A
150) C
151) A
152) C
153) B
154) D
155) D
156) C
157) B
158) D
159) C
160) A
161) C
162) C
163) D
164) C
165) B
166) B
167) C

168) E

169) B

170) D

171) C

172) C

173) C

174) B

175) B

176) D

177) C

178) C

179) E

180) B

181) B

182) D

183) C

184) B

185) B

186) C

187) C

188) A

189) B

190) B

191) D

192) C

193) A

194) C

195) D

196) C
197) C
198) E
199) C
200) B
201) B
202) D
203) B
204) C
205) B
206) C
207) C
208) D
209) D
210) C
211) E
212) B
213) C
214) A
215) B
216) C
217) C
218) A
219) A
220) E
221) C
222) A
223) C

224) C

225) C

226) D

227) A

228) C

229) B

230) C

231) D

232) A

233) C

234) D

235) B

236) B

237) D

238) E

239) B

240) C

241) D

242) D

243) D

244) C

245) C

246) C

247) D

248) E

249) E

250) B

251) D

252) B

253) A

254) D

255) D

256) A

257) C

258) C

259) B

260) A

261) E

262) B

263) D

264) A

265) B

266) B

267) D

268) E

269) C

270) E

271) C

272) D

273) C

274) A

275) C

276) D

277) E

278) D

279) A

280) C

281) D

282) D

283) B

284) C

285) C

286) D

287) E

288) D

289) C

290) D

291) C

292) D

293) C

294) C

295) E

296) D

297) A

298) B

299) B

300) E

301) E

302) C

303) D

304) E

305) B

306) C

307) C

308) D

309) B

310) E

311) B

312) D

313) C

314) D

315) B

316) D

317) B

318) B

319) B

320) A

321) A

322) A

323) A

324) D

325) B

APPLIED MATHEMATICS FORMULA SHEET

Weight

1 ounce ≈ 28.350 grams
1 pound = 16 ounces
1 pound ≈ 453.592 grams
1 milligram = 0.001 grams
1 kilogram = 1,000 grams
1 kilogram ≈ 2.2 pounds
1 ton = 2,000 pounds

Volume

1 cup = 8 fluid ounces
1 quart = 4 cups
1 gallon = 4 quarts
1 gallon = 231 cubic inches
1 liter ≈ 0.264 gallons
1 cubic foot = 1,728 cubic inches
1 cubic yard = 27 cubic feet
1 board foot = 1 inch by 12 inches by 12 inches

Distance

1 foot = 12 inches
1 yard = 3 feet
1 mile = 5,280 feet
1 mile ≈ 1.61 kilometers
1 inch = 2.54 centimeters
1 foot = 0.3048 meters
1 meter = 1,000 millimeters
1 meter = 100 centimeters
1 kilometer = 1,000 meters
1 kilometer ≈ 0.62 miles

Area

1 square foot = 144 square inches
1 square yard = 9 square feet
1 acre = 43,560 square feet

Circle

number of degrees in circle = 360°
circumference ≈ 3.14 × *diameter*
area ≈ 3.14 × (*radius*)^2

Triangle

sum of angles = 180°
area = ½ (*base* × *height*)

Rectangle

perimeter = 2(*length* + *width*)
area = *length* × *width*

Rectangular Solid (Box)

volume = *length* × *width* × *height*

Cube

volume = (*length of side*)^3

Cylinder

volume ≈ 3.14 × (*radius*)^2 × *height*

Cone

volume ≈ (3.14 × *radius*^{2} × *height*) ÷ 3

Sphere (Ball)

volume ≈ 4/3 × 3.14 × *radius*^{3}

Temperature

°C = 0.56(°F − 32) or 5/9(°F − 32)
°F = 1.8(°C) + 32 or (9/5 × °C) + 32

Electricity

1 kilowatt-hour = 1,000 watt-hours
amps = watts ÷ volts

www.ingramcontent.com/pod-product-compliance
Lightning Source LLC
Chambersburg PA
CBHW060424010526
44118CB00017B/2349